Laity's Mission in the Local Church

Laity's Mission in the Local Church

Setting a New Direction

Leonard Doohan

WIPF & STOCK · Eugene, Oregon

Wipf and Stock Publishers
199 W 8th Ave, Suite 3
Eugene, OR 97401

Laity's Mission in the Local Church
Setting a New Direction
By Doohan, Leonard
Copyright©1986 by Doohan, Leonard
ISBN 13: 978-1-5326-0857-5
Publication date 9/10/2016
Previously published by Harper & Row, 1986

A note to the new printing

This book was originally published in the late eighties, a time of renewal and excitement in the Church. Some of the hopes of that time have been realized, and others still need the generous response of all in the Church. Once again in our own generation a new spirit is stirring in the Church. We must overcome the failures of the past and prepare ourselves for a future of growth and responsibility. Let us rekindle spiritual insight, accept our spiritual destiny, and refocus on the essential teaching of our common baptismal responsibility. While many have left the institutional churches, and sadly may never return, perhaps the challenge to renewal of Pope Francis may re-attract them to the essentials of Christian commitment. The Church will grow and benefit from an informed laity who deepens knowledge of the essential teachings of faith. This book can remind us of the challenges we felt and can feel again. It can act as a reminder of our calling, and as an examination of what we have achieved and what still lies unfulfilled.

To
Sister Lillian Anderson, S.N.J.M.
Father Vincent Beuzer, S.J.
Sister Cara Lee Foley, S.N.J.M.
Father Armand Nigro, S.J.

Abbreviations of the titles of the documents of Vatican II:

B	*Bishops*	Decree on the Bishop's Pastoral Office in the Church
C	*Church*	Dogmatic Constitution on the Church
Co	*Communications*	Decree on the instruments of Social Communication
CT	*Church Today*	Pastoral Constitution on the Church in the Modern World
E	*Ecumenism*	Decree on Ecumenism
EC	*Eastern Churches*	Decree on Eastern Catholic Churches
Ed	*Education*	Declaration on Christian Education
L	*Laity*	Decree on the Apostolate of the Laity
Lit	*Liturgy*	Constitution on the Sacred Liturgy
M	*Missions*	Decree on the Church's Missionary Activity
NC	*Non-Christians*	Declaration on the Relationship of the Church to Non-Christian Religions
P	*Priests*	Decree on the Ministry and Life of Priests
PF	*Priestly Formation*	Decree on Priestly Formation
R	*Revelation*	Dogmatic Constitution on Divine Revelation
RF	*Religious Freedom*	Declaration on Religious Freedom
RL	*Religious Life*	Decree on the Appropriate Renewal of the Religious Life

Contents

Preface   ix

Chapter 1: Recent Developments Regarding Laity   1

Introduction, 1. Theological Developments Since Vatican II, 2. Influences in the Early 1980s, 7. Some Recent Beneficial Developments, 11. Current Negative Trends, 15. Some Areas of Hope, 20.

Chapter 2: Laity and the Local Church   24

Introduction, 24. Theology of the Local Church, 25. The Parish as Local Church, 31. The Local Church as Foundational Church, 37. Lay Responsibility in the Local Church, 41.

Chapter 3: Work   48

Introduction, 48. Approaches to Work: From Curse to Mission, 49. The Dignity of Human Work, 53. Work in Perspective: Leisure, 58. Work in a Lay-Centered Church, 63.

Chapter 4: Family   68

Introduction, 68. Family as Foundational Church, 69. Sexual Love and Life, 73. Parenting and Family Education, 77. The Importance to the Family of Conscience Formation, 81. Family Responsibilities in a Lay-Centered Church, 85.

Chapter 5: Outreach in Service and Social Involvement   90
Introduction, 90.   *Christianity and Social Consciousness*, 92.   *Service and Social Involvement*, 99.   *Christianity's World Vision of Justice*, 104.

Chapter 6: Celebration and Liturgical Life   110
Introduction, 110.   *Celebrating Life*, 111.   *Celebrating Prayer*, 115.   *Celebrating Community*, 119.   *Celebrating Worship*, 123.

Notes   128
Bibliography   138
Index   145

PREFACE

Recent years have witnessed a reemergence of interest in theology for laity, and this has been complemented by ever-increasing numbers of diocesan lay-ministry programs, specialized courses, renewal programs, and workshops. The Catholic Church has called for a special international Synod to discuss developments for laity since the Second Vatican Council, and other Christian Churches too have reassessed the roles of laity in their structures and ministry.

The continued decrease in the numbers of priests and religious also calls for prudent planning by Church administrators to involve laity so that Christian ministry may continue and the faithful may receive the services they need.

One of the notable characteristics of Christianity today is that it is less a Church-based religion and more a world-based religion. The ministries that people value most do not require ordination, and more and more these ministries are developed by committed laity in their daily lives.

In 1984 my book *The Lay-Centered Church* dealt with four aspects of a theological assessment of laity in the Church. First, I analyzed the models of laity current at the time, so that each of us might be more prudently aware of our own attitudes and biases in our approach to laity. Second, I evaluated developments in the Roman Catholic Church since the Council in areas of ecclesial responsibility, spiritual life, ministry, and pastoral practice. While focused on the Catholic Church, the assessment highlighted problems experienced by other Churches, too. The third aspect of the study was the presentation of an understanding of Church that had a lay dynamic to it, and I chose family. The last step in the theological reflection was to reread Church history and current trends in spirituality, and to do so from a lay point of view, noting that some positive developments in Church history have frequently led to negative side effects for laity.

The aim of *The Lay-Centered Church* was to stimulate reflection on the importance of laity at this critical time, and to urge that all Christians show a preferential option for laity in all Church decisions.

I do not seek a lay-controlled Church, but a lay-centered Church. We remain far from this, not because of a lack of commitment or vision, but frequently because of the immense pastoral problems met in implementing this hope. Large numbers of laity, including those who have accepted positions of responsibility in social, educational, healing, and administrative services, recognize their need for religious education. This present book on the mission of laity in the local Church focuses on the contribution of all laity to the life of the Church. Since that vision rarely filters down today, but rather percolates up to the universal Church, this book stresses the contributions of laity in their ordinary daily lives. However, it is a book that gives theological foundations for each of the aspects of lay life—foundations from recent Church teaching and practice. Each chapter offers a synthesis of Church positions before going on to identify the responsibilities of laity and their grass-roots contributions to the life of the Church.

Chapter 1 deals with developments in the life of laity since the early '80s, and thus picks up from the analysis of Chapter 1 in *The Lay-Centered Church*. Chapter 2 presents the theological basis for the conviction seen in the remainder of the book: that the focus of Church life today is local. The strength of the international Church depends upon the strength of small groups of lay Christians who are the foundation of the larger Church.

I then examine four major components of lay life: work, family, social service, and celebration. In each case I give a theological synthesis before analyzing the specific contributions of laity to the universal Church learned in these daily experiences.

I offer these reflections as a contribution to those dioceses, parishes, or individual laity who wish to focus on the essentials of their baptismal responsibilities in a lay-centered Church. I have brought together in one short text material that is generally scattered, and in each chapter have integrated both Church teachings and grass-roots lay contributions, thus bridging the frequent gap between Church teaching and lay hopes.

Church is primarily a local experience and reality. It is precisely at the local level where laity can contribute immensely. If they do so, the future of the universal Church will be very positive.

I would like to thank my wife Helen for her constant support of my work, our daughter Eve-Anne for her patience while I worked, and both for helping me keep right priorities in our life.

I have been particularly privileged to have Cyril A. Reilly of Winston • Seabury as editor for this book and for *The Lay-Centered Church*. His direction, suggestions, and challenge have bettered both books and have been a learning experience for me, and I take this occasion to express my gratitude and appreciation.

Chapter 1

RECENT DEVELOPMENTS REGARDING LAITY

Introduction

The hopes raised by the Second Vatican Council, such as those relating to greater participation by all the baptized in the life, structures, and liturgy of the Church, continue to appeal to many of the Christian faithful, especially the laity. Some of the crises provoked by the Council, such as those in authority, vocation, and ministry, have indirectly focused attention on laity and their contribution to the life of the Church. In fact, these years since the Council have seen a great reemphasis on the significance of laity to the present and future growth of the Church.

These post-Council times have produced, among other things, a mixture of hope and anger, a tension between a movement back to the past and a yearning for a changed future, and an emphasis on world peace while in the midst of theological warfare. The emergence of a variety of different ways of understanding and living as Church—a pluralism that embraces traditional and progressive interpretations—has underlined the reality that there is more than one Church in Roman Catholicism today.

There is no more a unified lay position than there is a unified clerical or religious community understanding of Church. The vast majority of laity have no particular interest in what happens in Church circles or theological dialogues, and continue their weekly socio-religious attendance at Church without that attendance having any necessary effect on or relevance to their lives for the rest of the week. This group of unconcerned and uncommitted Christians will continue to be the largest percentage of churchgoers in a religion that is now in the late stages of its development and no longer the small group with the prophetical challenge characteristic of its origins.

The post-Council decades have brought Roman Catholicism to an awareness that the whole Church will never be the same again. It could well be that a part of the Church will return to the way things used to be, but large numbers—particularly of laity, but of some religious and priests too—are moving steadily in a new direction. Our Church today is a lay-centered Church, and the focus of ecclesial commitment is the predominantly lay *local* Church.

In this first chapter, we will glance at the years since the Council to see the major developments in theology regarding laity. Second, we will examine a selection of major influences in the Church of the 1980s. Third, we will identify some of the recent developments that have had beneficial influence on lay life and some current negative trends. Finally, we will review areas of continued hope for the development of a lay-centered Church.

Theological Developments Since Vatican II

An Overview of Developments Regarding Laity's Role in the Church

The Council, which concluded on December 8, 1965, opened a new era in the life and mission of the universal people of God. For centuries, the Church had been practically equated with those five-tenths of one percent who managed and governed the Church, but the second Vatican Council gave renewed emphasis to the emerging role of the layperson. Early enthusiastic commitment of Church leaders produced many opportunities for laypersons to become involved in the life of the Church, such as those opportunities suggested in the conciliar documents on the Church and the Church in the Modern World; moreover, spiritual movements (Cursillo, Movement for a Better World, Marriage Encounter, to name a few) facilitated a new kind of national and international organization of laity and made many aware of how important those organizations were to Church life.

The first phase of commitment to the upgrading of the role of laity began to wane as we approached the end of the sixties. Questions were raised regarding what ought to be the direction of lay life and ministry. Many lost interest, and others returned to the emphases of pre-Council times or the earlier post-Council years.

By the mid-seventies, both laity and scholars of the theology of laity began to experience serious dissatisfaction and frustration regarding the specifics of the lay role and the theology underpinning the relationship of laity and hierarchy. The decade ended with concern and fear that post-Conciliar gains would be lost.[1]

The eighties have emphasized ministry and related questions. Much consideration has been given to the interrelationship of hierarchy and laity in Church ministry. Many laity have entered fulltime ministry, have served well and found profound satisfaction, but have also met problems of unjust salaries, absence of effective lay authority, and lack of clarification of their roles.[2]

During the mid-eighties, we began to feel the impact of decreased numbers of priests. Some dioceses merged parishes, others appointed religious as pastoral associates, and the people in the pews began to experience the reality of being a Church without enough priests.

The average Christian now can think differently than in the seventies. He or she is accustomed to married deacons, lay eucharistic ministers, and lay directors of religious education, youth services, pastoral counseling, budget, and plant management. As the faithful sit in the pews on a Sunday, they now hear reports from lay representatives of their parish organizations, and they elect fellow laity to positions of parish responsibility. And feminism is beginning to make significant impact on our experience and our thinking.

As we approach the end of the eighties and look back to the Council, we can be encouraged by its emphasis on the laity's life and mission in the Church. We can rejoice at the laity's new experience of Church with a more highly visible lay contribution. Though saddened by some negative developments, such as the decrease in numbers of priests and religious, laity can take satisfaction in the fact that many of their fellow lay Christians have stepped in to take over and have done very well.

Different Models of Lay Life

After an early post-Conciliar enthusiastic emphasis on the laity's life and role, we witnessed a substantial reduction in writings about laity. This seemingly unfortunate development was actually very positive, since it was caused by the rejection of the idea that the theology of laity was a discipline distinct from ecclesiology. Since the end of the seventies, the life and role of laity have been viewed almost exclusively in the context of ecclesiology.

The seventies and eighties have produced several ecclesiological syntheses.[3] Each way of understanding the Church implies a specific way of viewing lay life, mission, and ministry. Some of these ecclesiologies are expressed and studied, such as the understanding of the Church as sacrament or as herald. Others are implied in the ways people live out their awareness of the Church as servant or as community.

In order to deal with this variety of ecclesiological syntheses and to identify some common ground as a basis for future consensus, it has been common to speak of models of the Church.[4] Each model of Church gives concrete and specific interpretations to the role of laity. In other words, each model of Church is also a model of laity.

In my book *The Lay-Centered Church*, I studied extensively the ecclesiological trends of a quarter of a century and grouped together five models of lay life implied in the various approaches to Church.[5] I do not think other identifiable models have surfaced since the publication of *The Lay-Centered Church* in mid-1984.

The first of those five approaches to lay life sees the laity's role as one of instrumental ministry. Laity are seen to be instruments in the hands of the hierarchy, who are presumed in this model to have exclusively received mission and authority from Jesus. The second model sees laity as an ecclesial presence to the world. Inserted into secular situations, the laity are called to influence the world with Christ's message and in some way to be present to non-Christians in the name of the Church. The third model of laity interprets their role as one of world transformation and clearly emphasizes social responsibility, world transformation, and the fight against injustice. The fourth approach implies and calls for a restructuring of the Church. This theological position stresses collegiality and the priesthood of all the faithful, and is frequently experienced in basic ecclesial communities, team ministry, and intervocational work. The fifth model is the open-ended exploratory approach of many laity today, who courageously launch into new ministries and new forms of faith sharing. This heuristic model is rapidly becoming common in the lives of the vast majority of laity actively committed to some aspect of ministry on a full- or part-time basis.

Each of these five approaches can be specified even further with the additional insights of some current models of ministry.[6] Each approach is still extensively supported, but no one of them has obtained exclusive support. There are strengths and weaknesses in each. This pluralistic approach to lay life needs to move toward more common ground and greater unity. However, a greater spirit of openness and dialogue will be required from us all before we can identify a common understanding.

Beginnings of a Lay-Centered Church

Several models of the Church that have been suggested over recent years are difficult to understand, even for the professional theologian. Hence there has been a growing demand for an approach to Church that can be readily understood by all laity. In *The Lay-Centered Church*, I dedicated a chapter to searching for a

6 / LAITY'S MISSION IN THE LOCAL CHURCH

model of Church that was so clear enough the non-professional theologian could understand it, resonate with its inner challenge, know how to live its call, and feel competent to contribute to its development. I concluded by presenting the Church as family.[7] This same approach has been stressed by other writers and pastoral experts. Seeing the Church as family clearly has problems, inadequacies, and possibilities of role confusion. However, since the Church is a mystery, every interpretation will be inadequate. The emphasis on the Church as family is good not only because it is grounded in Scripture, Church tradition, and Conciliar documentation, but also and especially because it stresses qualities that every baptized person has, knows, and resonates with.

Not only can ecclesial life be seen as a way of life to which laity have much to contribute from their daily experiences and expertise, but also, Christian spirituality in general has been focusing more and more in recent years on aspects of life that are essentially lay, such as work, family life, and the dedication to peace and justice. We no longer see emphasized the extremes and at times oddities of spiritual life that we formerly saw in some approaches to religious life and obedience, or in rigorous physical penances, desert life, and in those who really become foolish for Christ: living on poles, in trees, or covered in mud. Withdrawal from the world and schizophrenic attitudes toward religious and world values are being replaced by involvement in world transformation and integration of the political and temporal into one's religious commitment. We are witnessing an underlining of our sense of common baptismal vocation, are becoming aware that life is grace, are renewing our commitment to the evangelical counsels, and are challenging one another to be open to the new priorities of Christian life as it dialogues with and interacts with the world.[8]

Finally, the whole movement in Christian ministry has identified over and over again that the priorities, needs, and hopes of people today—family development, parenting, personal fulfillment, education to intimacy, professional competence, group commitment to work for justice—are now largely being met by the committed layperson rather than by the cleric or religious.

To summarize: In the years since the Council, we have witnessed in the Church an effort to upgrade the image of all the baptized and to recognize their contributions as mature adults. We have also seen that in searching for clarification of the lay role, many approach the problem from different theological convictions, and their interpretations are consequently varied. We have also witnessed greater concern in ecclesiology, spirituality, and ministry to emphasize those qualities and values that are basic to all laity. Through all the ups and downs of these post-Council years, there is a constant effort to focus on the centrality of the laity's life and ministry.

Influences in the Early 1980s

Chicago Declaration of Christian Concern

Signed in 1977 by forty-seven prominent Catholics, the Chicago Declaration has continued to exercise forceful influence throughout the early '80s on theology regarding laity. The signers expressed profound concern at the growing tendency to view lay life and ministry as commitment to Church-related activities and to tasks traditionally assigned to clergy. "It is our experience that a wholesome and significant movement within the Church—the involvement of lay people in many Church ministries—has led to a devaluation of the unique ministry of lay men and women."[9]

The Declaration underlined that the unique ministry of laity was to be involved in the broader mission of the Church to the world. The laity's responsibility lies in "the service performed within one's professional and occupational milieu."[10]

Accepting the Council's insight that the secular nature of their lives is what characterizes laity, the signers lamented the decreased influence of Catholic lay organizations in professional life, the decrease in priestly leadership of laity in their secular ministry, and the takeover of areas of lay ministry by clergy and religious, as in political and social involvement.[11]

The Declaration called for laity who would "exercise their family, neighborly, and occupational roles mindful of their Christian responsibility."[12] The Church, it said, speaks to the world through responsible laity whose experience, political wisdom, and technical expertise can mediate the Gospel's call for peace, justice, and freedom.[13]

The response to the Chicago Declaration was not only immediate and overwhelming but has also been extensive and long-lived. In 1978, the National Center for the Laity was set up at Mundelein College as a clearinghouse for continued discussion on the prophetical challenge of the Declaration.[14]

A 1979 national interview of Catholic bishops confirmed the insights of the Declaration and concluded that laity are "invisible to the world" and that this absence of lay influence from social, political, and working life is "the single biggest problem facing the U.S. Church."[15]

The early years of the '80s have continued to produce the misguided understanding that a layperson's commitment means doing some kind of ecclesiastical service. The Declaration was wise in its concern and prophetical in its anticipation of the direction lay life could take.

Theology of Ministry

The most-emphasized topic in the early eighties is ministry. There have been some objections to this emphasis, for it seems an internal Church issue. It could be yet another dimension of the ecclesiastical narcissism of recent years and, further, could be precisely one of the approaches the Chicago Declaration condemned, especially if, as is frequently the case, ministry is understood to be services internal to the Church rather than services to the world. These objections are unfounded. In fact, this emphasis on ministry could also be seen as supporting the Declaration if lay ministry stresses service to the world. Moreover, the laity's exclusive involvement in secular situations, without any participation in the life of the official Church, could perpetuate a cleric-lay split. Furthermore, lay involvement in secular situations without ability to contribute to ecclesial policy-making would limit the laity's ability to determine which needs and which methods should be used to best achieve their prime purpose.

The research and reassessment of ministry in the late seventies and early eighties has been truly extensive and courageous. Many laity, unencumbered by the history of theology with its negative approach to laity, and by disciplinary practices that highlight the power of the clergy, have generously dedicated themselves to a variety of ministries of education, social services, and Church life. At the same time, theologians and historians have reassessed the history of ministry and found many forms of ministry in earlier ages; they have also found that certain ministries now considered standard or traditional are really of quite recent vintage.[16]

The ecclesiasticalization of ministry—that is, the gradual control over ministry, and the monopolizing of ministry by Church officials—and the linking of ministry and jurisdiction through Holy Orders is the result of a long political history and certainly does not reflect New Testament times. The desires of many laity to be involved in ministry are as much the result of the Spirit's inspiration as they were in apostolic times. The numbers of laity involved in ministry have reached such proportions that we now need to consider new ways to organize ministry,[17] and in the long run this could open new directions for restructuring the Church and exercising authority.

This ministry movement is bringing more and more laity into leadership positions in the Church. In the long run, it will produce a new understanding of Church among laity in general. Its influence in the eighties is very strong, and it will continue to be felt for many decades.

Ecclesiastical Documents

The Synod on the Family was held in Rome in 1980, and the *Apostolic Exhortation on the Family*, which resulted from the synod, was published in November 1981. John Paul II's great encyclical *On Human Work* was published in September of the same year.

The U.S. bishops' pastoral laity, *Called and Gifted: Catholic Laity 1980*, was presented in November 1980, and their pastoral on war and peace, *The Challenge of Peace: God's Promise and Our Response*, was published in May 1983. The new *Code of Canon Law* was promulgated in January 1983. In 1985 the early drafts of the bishops' pastoral on the economy appeared. The general guidelines in preparation for the special synod—were distributed in 1985.[18]

These are all exceptional documents, full of encouragement and challenge for laity. While we hope that their impact will be enormous, we must also be realistic in acknowledging that nowadays people rarely commit themselves to something they did not participate in. Of all those documents, only the bishops' pastorals on war and peace and on the economy received input from interested parties.

In his best-seller *Megatrends*, John Naisbitt spoke, among other things, of documented swings in social values from centralization to decentralization, from institutional help to self-help, from representative democracy to participatory democracy, from hierarchies to networking.[19] These reactions are also present in lay life today. Important positions are worked out locally by small groups who participate in the decisions and are therefore willing to carry them out. Effective parish councils, neighborhood support groups, and youth and women's groups take their directions from local needs and resources.

I am not suggesting that we do away with major ecclesiastical documents. Not at all! In particular, the ones listed are truly exceptional and merit dedicated study. However, it is with genuine sadness that we acknowledge that their influence will be negligible among laity. The most we can hope for is that the few who read them will eventually filter the insights to laity. And I do mean few, since most priests and religious will not read them either.

Experience consistently shows that pastoral letters and encyclicals are easily ignored. Perhaps the one document whose influence will be truly but indirectly felt is the new *Code of Canon Law*. Although worked out in seeming secrecy with practically no contribution from women religious or laity, the code with its strong control over clerics and religous will indirectly influence laity. The Code recognizes an unprecedented list of rights of laity,[20] acknowledges the need of lay ministry,[21] and insists on lay participation in Church government. However, effective power remains linked to ordination, and lay involvement in inner Church life is presumed to be consultative.[22] While the Code's influence will be real, it is not being welcomed as embodying the ecclesiology of Vatican II.

Some Recent Beneficial Developments

We see many positive developments in the Church of the early eighties regarding the greater integration of laity in the whole life of the Church. There have been continued efforts to decentralize the government of the Church and to humanize structures. New ways of living Christian discipleship have been emphasized, as in the spiritual movements and in the stress placed on a spirtuality of work or of family life. The dignity of all the baptized has been upgraded by focusing on the common identity, rights, and duties of all Christians and by challenging each person to assume responsibility for the Church's own life and for its outreach in mission and ministry, particularly in the lay context of family ministry. From among the many positive developments of recent years, I would like to highlight four that are especially significant for laity: a sense of baptismal vocation, a focusing on lay values, a commitment to participation in the life of the Church, and a reassessment of Church teachings and practices.

A Sense of Baptismal Vocation

Christianity used to be an inherited aspect of life, uniformly lived by entire families, cities, and even countries. Nowadays, faith is seen as a matter of personal choice, not an inherited tradition. It is a commitment one makes after becoming aware of what the responsibility of baptismal dedication implies. The Vatican Council II stressed the rooting of all vocations in baptism (C 30:1). In fact, the Council spoke of the equality of all members of the Church because of their baptism (C 32:2). There may be other vocations, such as those of priest and religious, but these are specific, not special. The special call of God to humankind is the call to baptismal commitment.[23]

There is a healthy awareness among a growing number of laity that their baptism implies that they are called to build a community of faith based on the word of the Lord and lived with a sense of gratitude and Christian liberty. Of course, many are uninterested and still live in a passive relationship to the local and universal Church. However, more and more laity are striving to be true to their baptismal vocation. They have given themselves enthusiastically to the life of the local Church in its educational, administrative, and service dimensions, and to its renewal of organizational, community, and liturgical life. They refuse to be put off by discouragement or by misdirection of energies or attempts to control or dominate them. Large numbers of laity, certainly more than all priests and religious combined, live as vital parts of a Church "from the roots"—a democratized, declericalized Church.[24]

A Focusing on Lay Values

The upgrading of the image of the layperson in recent years is due in part to a focusing on lay values in the Church. Laity have replaced priests and religious in many areas of ministry; some visible examples are primary and secondary education, adult education, sacramental preparation, and marriage counseling. And the new priorities of the Church's administrators are frequently in areas where laity have expertise, such as family life, social justice, politics, war and peace.

As ministry becomes more specialized, and as numbers of priests and religious decrease, laity are getting used to making their own decisions in matters of general education, sexual morality, and politics, especially in issues of peace and war.

The new emphases in Church ministry, emphases where laity have expertise personally and professionally, and the new approaches to discerning Christian teaching in morality within family, economic, and political contexts, together with a recentering of Church interests in lay values, inevitably lead, as they have in recent years, to a new look at the lay contribution to the Church.

Laity are not interested in clerical needs and issues. Rather, they bring the insights of Christianity to bear on "some very deep human experiences: sexuality, guilt, injustice, racism, womanhood, technology, institutions, global destruction vs global survival."[25] Laity know what is happening in the world and where the real challenges of Christianity lie.

The shape of the Church in each generation is generally determined by its response to society.[26] In previous generations that response has come from the hierarchy of the Church, but in our generation it is coming increasingly from the laity. Moreover, lay influence on the direction of the Church will surely increase in the years ahead, and the resulting image of the Church will be more and more lay-centered.

The way people live in any generation presumes an underlying theology and often becomes the basis for the future direction of the Church. These recent developments, mentioned above, clarify both how laity see themselves and in what direction the main body of the Church will possibly move.

A Commitment to Participation

In the years following the second Vatican Council, we have witnessed the wonderful development of spiritual movements, such as the Cursillo, Marriage Encounter, and various prayer groups, in which laity have learned to participate in religious sharing. These movements, found throughout the world, have drawn untold numbers of laity into an experience of community growth, faith sharing, sacramental life, and apostolic commitment. Referred to as the "lay pentecost" of our times, these experiences of participation in religious sharing are truly revolutionary.[27] Admittedly, these experiences have frequently been outside of local parish structures, but the clear desire for participation and involvement is very positive.

The increased involvement of laity in full-time and part-time ministry is a further indication of desire for participation in the life of the Church. Lay CCD coordinators, youth ministers, and liturgical coordinators are a relatively recent phenomenon. Possibly here too, as with many spiritual movements, local Church structures have not succeeded in channeling this lay desire for experience and participation; the result has been that groups committed to social justice, education, family life ministries, and so on, have developed outside the mainstream of Church life.

Even within local diocesan or parish structures, laity have generously given themselves to renewal, service, and planning. At times, their commitment has been firm even when realistic expectations were not encouraging.[28] Although confrontation attracts media attention, lay participation is largely characterized by a truly remarkable spirit of patience.

A new kind of lay person is emerging, neither fanatical nor extreme, but healthily committed and willing to struggle. If followers create leaders or get leaders they deserve, structural changes can also be anticipated in Church life.

A Reassessment of Church Teachings and Practices

More Christians are theologizing today than ever before. There are more creative scholars alive today than in the entire history of Christianity. Moreover, a large percentage of them are laity. And these scholars, whether clergy, religious, or laity, are developing new ways to do theology.

Many pastors and religious leaders are meeting problems, such as those in ministry, family life, and war, that the Church has never encountered in the same way before, and the answers of traditional theology no longer suffice. Religious leaders are struggling and searching for new ways to understand Christ's challenge in an ever-changing world.

Both pastors and scholars are not afraid to reevaluate Church history and to return to early inspiration without the historical, ecclesiastical, and political baggage of the centuries. Others simply start from the status quo, from the experiences of their own faithful community, and with nothing more than a general sensitivity to Christianity's past, try to respond faithfully in the present.

Many laity who never think explicitly of theology still theologize insofar as a theology underlies their commitment and vision. There is probably more theologizing in the Church today than at any other time in its history. There has been extensive rethinking of the nature of the Church, its necessary structures and channels of authority.[29] Scholars have delved into the communal character of the Church, its office-bearers, forms of ministry, and use of power.[30] Others have reexamined the nature of religious leadership and its effective use.[31]

These recent studies, a few of which we have mentioned, are producing new ecclesiological syntheses. Admittedly, some office holders operate out of an ecclesiology that does not allow them to accept many of the new developments, but for others the current reassessment of teachings and practices gives great hope.

Current Negative Trends

Divisions Within the Church

The Vatican Council, with its emphasis on the People of God, community, and service to the world, resulted in a changed understanding regarding the Church that led to polarization and its accompanying problems. The enthusiasm of 1965–1970 gave place to doubts, questions, frustration, and division.

The Church remains basically an unequal society, and the distinction, even separation, between laity and hierarchy is difficult to overcome, since it is so much a part of the historical experience of the Church. Vatican II's vision of the Church as a community in the midst of the world to serve the world could be attained only by common commitment to a shared vision, and this common commitment has not been possible because of the divisions we experience.

Early enthusiasm after Vatican II gave way to restlessness among many laity at the retention of the clear separation between clergy and laity. Meetings such as those in Detroit in 1976 and Chicago in 1981, together with the Roman Synod on the Family in 1980, although initiated for lay-hierarchy dialogue, actually openly manifested the gap that remains between many of the people and the governing body of the Church. This dualist concept of Church and ministry is portrayed even more vividly in that body's negative attitudes toward women.

A restricted sphere of Church life based on the sacrament of orders clearly leads to some valid distinctions. However, over history, these few clearly defined ministerial distinctions have snowballed into a clericalism that is false to the nature of the Church as the people of God.[32]

Protest against the concentration of power and control in the hands of so few continues to surface in the Church. Sometimes the protest is channelled to a specific topic such as the role of women. Sometimes it is seen in the increased number of drop-outs from Church life, or in a global rejection of ecclesiastical authority.

However, division between clergy and non-clergy is not the only manifestation of the polarization that followed the Council. Catholicism is not only an unequal society, but it now clearly has a two-party system.[33] The division between liberals and conservatives, progressive and traditional approaches, is now deep and is likely to remain. Many have been unwilling to accept any attempts at reform of theological positions and continue to take refuge in the comfort of religion. Catholic conservatism has become increasingly literalist and fundamentalist regarding papal and doctrinal positions. Liberal groups are equally firm in their positions, and it is inevitable that hostility will increase and that the two-party system will become a fixed feature for the immediate future.

Inflexibility of Structures

The Church's authority structures were ideal in some periods, but they are antiquated today.[34] Not only have we not seen any serious attempts at large-scale structural reform in recent years, but in fact we have seen an entrenchment in more conservative positions. The Dutch Synod in 1980 heralded the return to pre-Vatican II ecclesiology,[35] and the present Congregation for the Doctrine of the Faith has given indications of returning to former ways of conservatism and control. Many laity looked on with disgust at the treatment of Hans Küng, Edward Schillebeeckx, Robert Drinan, and Agnes Mary Mansour, the increase in the numbers of curial trials of theologians, and the return to secrecy in administrative practices.

Ecclesiastical authoritarianism and intransigence remain a scandal with which we will need to live, probably for many years. The possessive attachment to power and structures is unhealthy and generates increasing disrespect from growing numbers of active laity. It is difficult now to change the processes already in place, such as dominant hierarchical control, the equating of Catholicism with the magisterium, the centuries of disregard of the laity, the constant exclusion of women, and the narrow views of sin.

Some structures in the Church are the unfortunate result of problem periods of history. What the concentration of power in the pope actually means or should mean for the Church today is not all that clear.[36] Moreover, not only bishops, but other persons too have shared and can share in the Church's magisterium.[37] Even the very opposition of the Christian faithful to Church law has in the past eventually become the dominant praxis and in the end been sanctioned by the official Church.[38]

To criticize the current lay opposition to the inflexibility of ecclesiastical structures and to the oppressive power and control they exercise is to show a lack of appreciation of both history and theology, for there have been times when lay leadership was crucial to maintain orthodox teaching,[39] and the laity's "non-acceptance of law" is an important guiding principle for correct teaching.[40] Listening to the consensus of the faithful has a solid basis in our theological heritage.

Many laity's dissatisfaction with a hierarchical ecclesiology is not a superficial request for democracy. There are some minimum elements of Church life and order that are possibly traceable to Jesus, such as overseers, imposition of hands, community judgment, and so on. It is not this aspect of structure that is questioned, but rather all the other man-made features of the Church that can and possibly should be changed, such as the centralizing of power, the mimicking of political governments by office-holders, the use of control, and the primacy of law. Dulles speaks of "the dissatisfaction of the Catholic intelligentsia" and of the Church's failure "to propose an alternative image."[41] Schillebeeckx speaks of "urgently required alternative possibilities" and says they are "bound to be regarded as at least temporarily illegal."[42]

We need to see clear signs of a willingness to change those structures that have no theological claims to permanence. At times, some of our current structures seem to be suppressing the very values they were developed to uphold. The evidence of lack of religious education among so many, the polarization in our Churches, and the general lack of respect for clergy show beyond question that the system is ineffective and should be changed. Lay initiatives in calling for a new style of authority will need to be courageous, since attempts of this kind are quickly labeled "heretical" or "unorthodox." However, this attempt to control by labels and by laws written by those in power is itself one of the undesirable features of our Church structures.

Unmet Needs of Laity

We have never had a lay-centered Church.[43] This fact has produced and continues to produce many unmet needs for the people of the Church. Laity need to be valued for who they are as members of the Church and not merely for what they might be able to do to relieve a shortage of professional ministers. Many are drifting away from a faith that does not seem able to meet their daily needs. Dulles claims: "The Catholic Church seems unable to capitalize on the yearning for religious commitment and spiritual experience by so many of our contemporaries."[44] Religion is significant to them; so too is Church. But a Church with innumerable structures, laws, and office holders is for many an unnecessary obstacle.

For many of those laity who continue to live within the Church's structures there is a growing anger at cosmetic change, such as an occasional consultation with laity, while real dialogue, power, and authority are withheld from them. The resulting restlessness of laity at times leads to the coexistence of two Churches.

The double problem of parallel Churches and parallel structures of ministry that we now have within Catholicism is complicated by the growing failure to provide sacramental ministers for the people, the refusal to deal with women's issues, the poor religious education of many Roman Catholics, the inadequacy of spirituality for the modern world,[45] and the lack of good updated post-Conciliar theology in many Church officials who are still left in control.[46]

Laity need to be asked what kind of Church they want. This does not mean the loss of the basics of our faith, since laity are clearly as competent to safeguard essentials as clergy are. The elitist descending ecclesiology of recent centuries is totally unsuitable for today. It is discouraging to laity to constantly be contributing more and more financial assistance for programs they see as doomed to fail. When the enormous budgets for seminary training are compared with the meager budgets for lay formation it is difficult to see what can justify this disparity.

In spite of administrators' unwillingness to meet basic lay needs, and a continued disregard of fundamental rights to dialogue and discussion,[47] many generous laity remain committed to a structured Church, hoping their sacrifice will bear fruit. Dolores Leckey, addressing the laity's needs, identifies the following: the need of places and opportunities to tell the truth; the need to know they have been listened to and heard; the need for opportunity to minister; the need to have the ordinary worldly ministry of the laity affirmed; the need for support of their vocation through theological education and spiritual formation.[48]

Obviously, laity are not the only ones whose needs remain unanswered. Priests and religious frequently feel in the same position. Moreover, on all sides there is goodness and dedication; certainly blame for the current position cannot be assigned to anyone in particular. However, the paralysis we are in is quite frightening and is certainly one of the current reasons for concern.

Some Areas of Hope

Ecclesial Coresponsibility

The Vatican Council reminded all of us that we were entering a new age in human history (CT 54:1). This new age, which is characterized by constant change, has also provoked a serious crisis for Catholicism, possibly one of the gravest crises in the entire history of the Church. In times of crisis, it is common to exert every effort to preserve what we have. However, the current crisis is not one of fidelity but of relevance. The task is not to close ranks to protect what we have, but to be creative in reincarnating Christianity in the late twentieth century.

The people of the Church have a growing sense of coresponsibility. Bishops, pastors, and religious are working with the people. However, this spirit of collaboration needs to increase not only for efficiency but also as a manifestation of the faith we profess. Only when we realize together the collective gifts of our baptism can we show today's world the greatness of Christianity.

Ecclesial coresponsibility is best seen at the level of the local

Church, through collaborative efforts in team work, intervocational ministry, parish and diocesan pastoral councils, and shared authority. In some parishes and dioceses we see decentralization of administration, greater participation by some of the people, and development of networking among committed Christians (when several small groups each relate to the others without any hierarchical organization). The continued growth of small local groups, or basic communities, often with a dimension of outreach, is a further sign of ecclesial coresponsibility.

The growing number of laity who are now training for Church ministry, together with all the current ecclesial ministers in religious education, parish schools, social work, youth ministry, and parish and diocesan administration, indicate a sense of coresponsibility. This is even clearer when we realize that all these lay ministers have sacrificed much to pay for their own education, and continue to sacrifice by accepting poor salaries. What they do is not simply a job, for they could get better pay elsewhere; rather it is ministry coming out of a sense of responsibility for the Church.

These developments are showing us that we have within us the gifts we need to be the Church the eighties and nineties need. They are also the early signs of a lay-centered Church, where equality of discipleship is evident. This growing spirit of coresponsibility is truly one of the present areas of hope.

Prophetical Community

In the Church of the last two decades we have seen all kinds of effort to build community. Large numbers of the people have attended workshops, retreats, renewal programs, and other group meetings. There has also been extensive development in prayer groups, family-life encounters, and faith-sharing groups. Many parishes now have specialists in youth ministry, family life, adult education, music, and liturgy. There has been not only a lot of struggle but also substantial success. The spirit of community, while usually restricted to only a part of the local Church, is still a very positive development of recent years.

In addition to the efforts to build community, theologians and ecclesiologists have drawn out the implications of these community developments for local Church life, government, ministry, and worship.

The new attitudes among the different vocations are also a healthy contribution to community growth. Priests and religious are treated as humans, rather than being placed on a pedestal. They in turn treat laity with increased respect and appreciation.

Even the design of our more recent church buildings portrays a sense of community. Our local Church community centers and social programs are further indications of community growth.

All this comes at a time of social unrest, war, division, and polemics at every level of society. At a time when the world is crying out for love, friendship, and community, we see the Church struggling to develop within itself and portray to others the value of these very qualities.

There is a prophetical dimension to the current Church emphasis on community. It is a faithful portrayal of oneness in Christ (see Gal. 3:27–28). It is also a vision and challenge to those who consider change in our present world impossible. True community, with all its demands and implications, offers a new type of society to a hate-filled world and "is in harmony with the most secret desires of the human heart" (CT 21:8).

The problems faced since the Council produced an identity crisis for the Church. And it is difficult to challenge the world when the Church itself is so divided. Nevertheless, these initial efforts at community growth are not only healing for the Church but also give it an ability to proclaim its message to others with credibility. In struggling to build community, the Church is giving an interpretation to the meaning of life, an interpretation that sees all members as integral parts of the common life.

Patient Hope

When many laity look at themselves as Church in the eighties, they often seem to be on the border between hope and despair.

There are many positive developments and yet many reasons for concern. On the one hand, the reemphasis on baptismal vocation, the renewed importance of the lay values of life, the greater participation of laity in Church life, and a willingness to reassess Church teachings have generated a sense of hope. On the other hand, the continued divisions, inflexibility of structures, and unmet needs of laity continue to provoke a feeling that major elements of Church life will never change.

The Bible itself is an education to hope, as it shows us the constant fidelity of a God who is drawing us to himself. And just as the biblical periods of crisis and destruction heralded new life, our problems in the Church today can lead to new life if we deal with them in a spirit of ecclesial collaboration.

Living in the Church today, with its many problems, requires great patience—a patience permeated with hope. We see this hope not only in the struggle-filled lives of religious and priests, but also in the endurance of laity. The euphoria of the Council years soon passed, and we now daily face the hard struggles of Church renewal. The clash of personalities, the oppression of institutions, the inflexibility of laws, the insistence on rank and office are all still with us. Some laity have left the institutional Church; others remain as passive Sunday worshippers. The nonviolent opposition of some, the ecclesiastical disobedience of others, and the patient dialogue of yet others all contribute to the struggle in faith and hope.

These difficult years are making us people of tomorrow, people of patient hope. The Council, in a fine text, called for such hope-filled people. "We can justly consider that the future of humanity lies in the hands of those who are strong enough to provide coming generations with reasons for living and hoping" (CT 31:4).

The patient hope of these years is a necessary component of lay spirituality. We need to be patient enough to give one another time, to forgive, to forget, and to try again, and hopeful enough to be courageous, self-critical, and confident that we can become a Church relevant for the '80s and '90s.

Chapter 2

LAITY AND THE LOCAL CHURCH

Introduction

In 1963–1965, the universal Church was gathered in Rome for the Second Vatican Council. Paul VI, in his closing speech, called it the largest, richest, and most opportune Council in the history of the Church. In his first encyclical, John Paul II spoke of the immense work of the Council as being directed toward the rooting in all of us of "that full and universal awareness" of what it means to be Church.[1]

The leadership of recent popes and bishops, especially since John XXIII, has been complemented by the growth in ecclesial awareness fostered by spiritual movements, theologians, and outstanding clergy, religious, and laity. The insights and renewal efforts of all these individuals and groups are powerful manifestations of the guidance of the Holy Spirit in our times. For all Christians today, conversion, more than ever before, is a conversion to be Church.

The way we understand Church conditions what we think conversion implies and calls us to. Not only are there several models of Church, each emphasizing specific components of spirituality, but we can also understand the Church as universal, national, regional, diocesan, parochial, and possibly as on other levels too, each level requiring certain attitudes from participants. The Church is a rich reality that challenges us in many ways. There are challenges in appreciating and in living the institutional aspect of the Church. There are other challenges when we attempt to live out the Church's vision of true community. In fact, the many ways of living as Church also satisfy the different psychological needs of the human person.

Out of the many suggested models of Church, each generation tends to emphasize the one model that generates confidence as the current best way of understanding and explaining the Church. The major models, or paradigms, of the last twenty years have provoked attitudes and courses of action for the faithful. Understanding the Church as herald or as community requires different attitudes. In each case the model calls for a specific kind of conversion.

The approaches of the last twenty years were valuable, but they were pastorally deficient. Something else was needed. Because they were all deductive, descending ecclesiologies (by which I mean understandings of the Church presented by Church officials or theologians and passed down to the faithful), they were meaningless to the average baptized Christian. Such Christians may give the impression of following one model or other, but their priorities and convictions are different from those of the Church official or theologian. By the time deductive, "from above," descending ecclesiologies reach the grass roots, they are not relevant or even understandable, and most laity are not committed to any of them.[2]

The focus of Church life today is local: where laity live, participate, create vision, and foster commitment. The ecclesiologies for today are basically inductive; they start at the grass-roots level with the local life of the Church. Here at the local level, faithful laity cannot only maintain the valuable insights of our traditions and preserve respect for the ministries of Church official or theologian, but can also make their own unique contribution to the Church, a contribution that percolates up to the advantage of the universal Church.

Theology of the Local Church

The Concept of Local Church in Vatican II

The Vatican Council complemented its own emphasis on the universal Church with a significant section on the local Church, inserted after major interventions of the Greek and Eastern bishops.

Number 26 of the document on the Church gives us a fine theology of the local Church. "The Church of Christ is truly present in all legitimate local congregations of the faithful, which, united with their pastors, are themselves called churches in the New Testament" (C 26:1). These local communities, united with their bishop or pastor, are not equal to part of the universal Church; rather, the local Church is the incarnation or concrete expression of the universal Church in its highest form. "In these communities, though frequently small and poor, or living far from any other, Christ is present. By virtue of Him the one, holy, catholic, and apostolic Church gathers together" (C 26:2). What can be affirmed in faith of the universal Church can be affirmed of these local expressions of the Church. It is precisely when we look at these small, poor, local communities that we catch a glimpse of the beauty, richness, and greatness of the Church. Moreover, it should be stated explicitly that these communities are to be *in union with* their bishop or pastor. The document does not state that the bishop or pastor is present or needs to be present.

The insights of this paragraph of the document on the Church are complemented by several other references to the local Church. Admittedly, the focus of the Council is the local diocesan Church, sometimes called a particular Church,[3] "in which the one, holy, catholic, and apostolic Church of Christ is truly present and operative" (B 11:1). The bishop fashions his local Church on the image of the universal Church in such a way that "in and from such individual Churches there comes into being the one and only Catholic Church" (C 23:1).

The focus in the Council is primarily on the particular diocesan Church and not on organizations greater or smaller than it. Nevertheless, there are some indications of further decentralization of the concept of Church. Speaking about priests in their pastoral ministry, the Council says, "They make the universal Church visible in their own locality" (C 28:3), and it challenges the priests to "so lead and serve their local community that it may worthily be called by that name by which the one and entire People of God is distinguished, namely, the Church of God" (C 28:6). Missionaries are also urged to form local Christian communities that truly embody the life of the universal Church (M 15).

The concept of local Church, then, refers specifically to the particular diocesan Church. However, in the broad sense it can also refer to other Christian groupings such as the parish, which represents "the visible Church as it is established throughout the world" (Lit 42:1), and even religious orders and basic ecclesial communities.[4]

This concept of local Church is taken even a step further by the Council when it speaks of the domestic Church (C 11:5; CT 48:8). In the early Church, the diocese and later the parish were the primary foundational cells of Church life, but now they no longer are. These larger institutional groupings are secondary expressions of basic Church life. The Council spoke of the family as a domestic Church. Even though theologically it has many meanings, *family* is often restricted to marriage. Better by far is the approach of Pope John Paul II, who refers to these small cells of ecclesial life as the foundation of Church[5] and sees them as constituting the Church in its essential dimension.[6] If ecclesial life is not strong in the basic and primary group cells of local Church, it cannot be strong at any other level. What is presumed is "a view of the Church from below, where component communities of the wider Church are seen as establishing the foundation for the Church's life."[7] Whatever is built on this foundation of local Church life will be strong or weak depending on the strength or weakness of this foundation.

The Council in its teaching on the local Church strongly underlines the importance of local Church life and challenges to a conversion at that level.[8]

The Relationship Between Local Church and Universal Church

Our Church is actualized at both the local and the universal levels. The relationship between the two levels produces mutual growth. However, the prime embodiment of Church is at the local level. Here is the foundation on which the universal Church is built. It is possible to have growth in the local Church that contributes to the upbuilding of the universal Church. However, it is not possible to have growth at the universal level without its being a manifestation of local foundational Church growth.

Local Church is Church, but not the whole Church. It manifests the Church but does not exhaust that reality.[9] In fact, the local Church is not totally independent or autonomous. Rather, it needs a dynamic interrelationship with other communities of the universal Church for its own growth and fulfillment.

The universal Church is a communion of local Churches and does not have an existence independent of them. Pope John Paul II stated: "The perfect identity of the local churches is to be found in complete openness to the universal Church."[10] It is likewise true that the perfect identity of the universal Church is to be found in complete openness to the local Churches.

In the past, the international dimension of the Church was given more importance than its local dimension. Nowadays, Church is thought of as primarily local, and the international dimension is of less significance. This is true even on a government level. Who the top officials of the international Church are does not matter to people the way it used to. The leader of the local Church is more significant, because it is here where growth will be fostered or stunted. As Naisbitt correctly states, "Hierarchies remain; our belief in their efficacy does not."[11]

In the past, power was concentrated in a few top officials of the international Church. Nowadays, that power is less effective and is more frequently questioned. Church structures tend to follow political types, and Church officials, like all hierarchies, tend to be committed to the system and structure of which they are a part. Generally, the higher a person is in a hierarchy, the more committed he or she is to preserving it, and the less willing he or she is to change it.[12]

Local Churches can be a corrective to the inherent defects of hierarchical power, such as structural preservation, attitudes of dominance, narrow views of truth, triumphalism, and power linked to status and shown in a desire to control. All power is for service, and through interaction with the local Church it can be appreciated that all service is mutual and all authority is mutual. The universal Church best portrays its own identity when it is truly a collegial expression of the life, teachings, and vision of the local Churches. In the past, theological positions usually filtered down to the local Churches, though history documents some notable exceptions; now, for the most part, they percolate upwared to the universal Church.[13] This change requires a new sense of responsibility in the local Church and a new style of administration in the universal Church.

We find ourselves in a period of swings in theology: from office to charism, from jurisdiction to service, from official Church to a Church of the people, from an international uniformity to a pluralistic community, from hierarchy to people, from universal Church to local Church. These are not either/or positions, but both/and. Nevertheless, the reality most emphasized is the life of the local embodiment of Church life. International Church officials facilitate the growth of the universal Church when they lead the many local Churches into deeper communion with one another.

Leadership for the local Church

When we look at the Church of the eighties, any creative developments in leadership, team leadership, and new structures of leadership are in local Churches. It is unrealistic to expect that such developments would take place on an international level, since the higher one is in a hierarchy, the less likely one is to change it. The integration of charismatic leadership and institutional leadership, the recognition of new effective ministries, and the growth in appropriate spiritual renewal take place principally at the local level.

Some of these efforts would probably not be accepted by international church officials. Schillebeeckx speaks of "a wave of alternative praxis and this in itself is a clear indication that the existing order in the Church has lost its credibility and is in urgent need of revision."[14]

It is at the local level where we have laity in administrative positions, on councils, and in teams. It is in some local Churches that we have laity directing diocesan or parish offices, working on major budget planning, teaching in seminaries. It is in local Churches that laity are leaders of spiritual renewal, prayer movements, and faith sharing. It is at the local level that laity spearhead education, social reform, and marriage encounter. In some local Churches, where priests, religious, and laity collaborate, vocational distinctions are not clear-cut, and office and leadership are not immediately thought of as identical.

Leadership in the local Church is more flexible, shows mutual intervocational appreciation, and is the first level at which laity are integrated into the life of the Church. However, when local Church is seen as the foundation of the universal Church, then this is the basic level, since all the rest of the Church is built on this.

Moreover, recall that the concept of local Church can be applied to small communities, even to the domestic Church, the family. In fact, only these are truly foundations of the Church, since they alone are prime groups. Here laity are the major even though not the only leadership figures.

The Council's teaching on local Church emphasized the importance of the lay contribution at the local level of diocese, parish, community, and family. While these local Churches are related to the universal Church, they are themselves the prime ecclesial reality. This is very significant and challenging for laity. Furthermore, when we look at the local Church we see new approaches to leadership that capitalize on lay expertise and commitment: collegial, democratic, or charismatic forms of leadership, situational leadership learned in professional life, cell or group leadership from industry, mutual leadership from family life, and servant leadership from civic and social life.

The Parish as Local Church
The History and Importance of the Parish

As I have pointed out, Vatican II's theology of the local Church centers on the diocese but leaves the door open for application of the notion to other groups within the diocese. The prime local Church, which is the foundational experience of Church, is now the basic community, often a family or neighborhood group, made up of no more than about twelve persons. Nowadays, for psychological and sociological reasons, we emphasize small groups, but the early Church too had emphasized home Churches and followed the Jewish practice of allowing every group of twelve families to have its own leader.[15]

By the fourth century there were many overseers, or bishops, of these small Churches. Gradually the more important and better-educated city bishops began to exercise control over the rural bishops whom they had ordained in the first place. After Constantine (d. 337), the numbers of bishops decreased, and by the time of Leo I (440–461) small communities no longer had a bishop as their leader, but a priest.[16]

Paralleling this local reorganization was the development of the diocesan structure of the Western Church. A diocese was a regional district of the Roman empire; after Constantine the Church gradually adopted a similar districting in ecclesiastical matters, and powerful bishops emerged as ecclesiastical governors over the Roman diocesan regions.

At first the bishop retained all sacramental and jurisdictional power in his diocese. After the increased freedom given to Christians by Constantine in the Edict of Milan (313), Church membership increased, and the needs of the faithful could no longer be supplied by the bishop alone. The numbers of Churches increased, and some of them became the center of local religious life and had resident priests who were given authority to preach and baptize.

The strength and independence of these local Churches grew with the expansion of the Church and its increased financial security. The local parishes gradually became centers of social and religious activities. The territorial distinction that is part of a parish became a general practice only with the Council of Trent (1545–63). Moreover, prior to Trent, laity had often elected their pastors and administered Church property, but after Trent the laity were placed in subordinate and passive roles.[17]

The Second Vatican Council speaks of the parish as the most important example of a local Church within the diocese (Lit 42:1). The Council sees the parish as a local embodiment of the diocesan Church and urges the priest, "who takes the place of the bishop" (Lit 42:1), to foster the parish's close relationship to the bishop (Lit 42:2).

The parish was an outstanding development in bringing the Church to local people. It was, and remains, the place where most people encounter Church and become Church. In origin it was a clear sign of the decentralization of the diocese.

In earlier times, dioceses were much smaller, and bishops governed far fewer persons than a typical pastor does today. Parishes are no longer prime groups nor even communities. They are in most cases too large and have too few ministers to run them. The very establishing of parishes in the early centuries was a response to that kind of situation, and as we examine the changing role of the parish today, it seems inevitable that the Church, to remain alive and lifegiving, will need to do again what it did in the past: further decentralize and grant sacramental and jurisdictional powers to others who previously did not exercise them.

The Changing Role of the Parish

Since the '70s, the parish has changed immensely and has lost its central importance. There are many reasons for this. Social developments (such as the anonymity of the neighborhood, the mobility of job seekers) and changes in family life (such as the need for one of the partners to take two jobs, weekend vacationing away from the parish, single-parent families with different needs, and divorced persons who feel rejected by the parish) have had serious repercussions on parish life. People's religious needs are different from what they used to be, and as a consequence the ministry of the parish has changed. Furthermore, the Vatican Council called both priest and parishioners to new styles of participation in the local Church: collaboration, coresponsibility, and liturgical participation, to mention a few. Moreover, we now live in an unstable, urbanized world with a technological culture, an anonymous society, and uprooted families. The population is mobile and has a variety of value systems. Faith used to be inherited and supported in the local parish by collective attitudes to devotions, and was aided by parish schools, hospitals, colleges, and many other religious institutions. Now faith is the result of a personal decision and grows through personal search. The religious character of many hospitals and colleges is gone, and even the local parish school is carefully evaluated alongside state schools to see if it gives the best education that parents can offer their children.

For our grandparents, parish life was an automatic choice, but now laity choose their parish carefully, even traveling across town if necessary. Moreover, people today have fewer expectations of the parish. There are many specialized organizations outside the parish, with better-salaried and therefore often better-qualified personnel. If people desire individual, family, or marriage counseling, adult education, aids to community growth, answers to religious questions, or even help in prayer or spiritual direction, chances are they will answer their needs outside the parish structure.

In previous decades the pastor held a role of undisputed authority. In fact, it was normal to grant authority to age, experience, tradition, and institution. But now, more and more, authority is being given to education, competence, adaptability, and creativity. Without these qualities the pastor often finds himself without the respect he once had. This situation is intensified by the emergence of well-qualified religious and laity, who provoke in the parish priest a sense of insecurity.

While people may go elsewhere to satisfy their needs, the pastor obviously feels responsible for the people in his parish and wishes to bring Christ to them in their need. However, in doing so, the pastor finds himself involved in ministries his predecessors did not have to the same extent—a situation the Vatican Council had anticipated (P 1:3). He must deal with many unmarried, sexually active younger people, with pregnancies, contraception, and abortion. He may have a major ministry to the separated and divorced. He ministers to people who only partially identify with the Church. He may see himself forced to satisfy people's social needs rather than their religious needs. He finds himself called to develop ministries to, for, and by older people, the unemployed, or early retired.[18]

The Vatican Council called for greater participation by laity in the life of their local parish. The Council states that pastors were never intended to shoulder all parish responsibilities. Rather they should work with the laity and identify the gifts the laity can contribute to parish life. Pastors are called to promote the dignity of laity, enter into dialogue with them, give them opportunity to freely express their opinions, and to follow up on their suggestions. Pastors should willingly assign duties to the laity and let them undertake tasks on their own initiative. After all, the Council concludes, laity are essential to local Church, and they should be encouraged to collaborate energetically in all parish projects.[19]

All this has led to a new understanding of the parish, an appreciation of its reduced importance since the seventies, and an awareness of new styles of pastoral leadership.[20]

The Future of the Parish

Some dioceses have reorganized their parish structure. There are now super-parishes made up of several traditional parishes; there are ministry teams that direct several parishes; there are parishes organized by deacons; and there are religious women or laity who are pastoral associates. This experimentation is the result of the shortage of priests.

Recent studies have also shown that there are some very successful parishes that parishioners find alive and active, committed to a sense of ministry, healing, and outreach, organized democratically with community involvement, and offering opportunity for relevant spiritual growth.[21]

Those successful parishes have a clear vision of what it means to be local Church, a strong corporate commitment, and a collegial style of administration. Similar needed qualities were identified in the interim report of the U.S. bishops' committee on the parish. The report confirmed that there is no real parish renewal without an emphasis on new structures of leadership, community involvement in liturgical life, structured groups for spiritual growth, and a sense of mission and ministry.[22]

In the short run, however, it is difficult to be optimistic. Super-parishes seem artificial and specifically designed to cope with the shortage of priests while still keeping the priests in charge. The reduced number of priests can expect to carry a double workload. "Each suburban pastor now working without an associate priest will have to add another parish to his responsibilities as we move into the 1980s."[23] Even if we keep full churches, it seems inevitable that we will have empty rectories. Unless we rethink the nature of the priesthood, it seems likely that new local structures will develop to satisfy the people's needs, with parishes remaining only where priests are able to develop a local Church where laypersons play their rightful role.

Such parishes will be characterized by satisfying religious experiences, broad-based participation in the Church's life, and a truly collaborative approach to faith. They will be parishes that laity can truly acknowledge as their own.

Perhaps the prime need that people hope the local Church will answer is a satisfying religious experience and a meaningful religious celebration of one's daily life. This is very difficult to facilitate in large Churches of mixed communities, where people are at different levels of identification with the Church. What is meaningful to one is not to another, and parishioners need to select from the parish experience whatever, in their judgment, is going to be conducive to faith development.

Parishioners do not *belong* to their Church; they *are* their Church. It must be in a local group that they find fulfillment, common vision, solutions to their religious questions, and respect for who they are. It needs to be a group they can truly acknowledge as their own, an extension of themselves. In fact, "the way a local church organizes its common life says far more about what it believes than all that it teaches and preaches."[24]

We have seen that no one acknowledges as their own what he or she does not participate in. Parishioners with a sense of coresponsibility should participate in all major decisions that significantly affect their corporate life: liturgy, community life, finance, allocation of Church resources, choice of pastor and of Church ministers. This participation should also include parish input on diocesan issues that affect the parish in its spiritual life, finance, pastoral planning, choice of bishop, and evaluation of all ministers in their pastoral performance.

Parishes that remain will assume responsibility for themselves and will manifest a truly collaborative approach to faith, discerning together what forms Christianity should take in their locality. This approach will include serious corporate commitment to the study of the faith, and parish theologizing and interpreting of faith for their own environment and time. It will mean corporate commitment to ministry that makes the parish a ministering Church.

The future of the local Church is not going to be like that of the traditional parish. A reduced number of parishes will remain, but a glance at their strengths will indicate that they will really be communities of communities. Ideally, it is not primarily the parish that gives life to the people; rather, people who have found life elsewhere in small groups give life to the parish. As Jürgen Moltmann says, "My thesis is a simple one: The local congregation is the future of the church. The renewal of the church finally depends upon what happens at the grass roots level."[25] The parish of the future will be a secondary group that celebrates this strength of the local communities that constitute it.

The Local Church as Foundational Church

The Family: Church in Miniature

We are a people of faith, and so we will always be called and challenged by a descending ecclesiology, a call "from above," from the pastoral leaders of the Church. However, the Church is necessarily a local expression of life, and we have seen how the Vatican Council complements our understanding of the universal Church with its teachings on the centrality of the local Church. The particular expression of local ecclesial life is the diocese, whose life, call, and mission are made present in parish life. The parish, however, is not the foundation of the Church. In fact, it cannot be, because it is itself composed of a multiplicity of other groups that give it strength or predetermine its weaknesses. Among these foundational expressions of Christian life, primacy belongs to the family grouping. Admittedly, the word *family* is applied by the Council to a wide range of small ecclesial groups whose members are bound together by love, common vision, and commitment to one another.[26] However, its principal meaning is the traditional bonded group of close relatives. Vatican II calls this family unit "the domestic Church" (C 11:5; L 11:4) and sees it "as a reflection of the loving covenant uniting Christ with the Church" (CT 48:8). When Christ's call is lived within this foundational cell of Church, the family can "manifest to all . . . the genuine nature of the Church" (CT 48:8).

Two emphases of the Council are significant here. The Church as a whole is called to live as a family, and the family is called to live as a domestic Church. "There is a natural and foundational interrelationship between family and Church in their essence and in their prime values. Church happens at the level of the family; if it does not develop there, then its presence at any other level of the Church, though possible, is always exceptional."[27]

These small family cells of ecclesial life are the basic manifestations of local Church. The strength of the Church in the years ahead will principally depend upon laity's ability to form Church within the context of their local lives. We will have a lay-centered Church or face the growing irrelevance of Christianity.

Unfortunately, the domestic Church has not become as strong as the Council hoped it would. It is frequently passive and unwilling to accept its responsibilities. The leadership and guidance of outstanding laity, religious, and clergy have achieved a lot, and the family movements have done an outstanding job. But the task ahead is great, and unless increasing numbers of families live their responsibilities as domestic Church, we must anticipate a weakened Church in parishes and dioceses.

Basic Ecclesial Communities

Since the late sixties we have witnessed the wonderful development of another form of foundational Church in addition to the family: the basic ecclesial communities. These small groups are the "germ-cells" *(Keimzelle)* of ecclesial life in the Third World and also in many cities of North America. These predominantly lay groups are one of the finest expressions of the growth and vitality of contemporary Christianity. They have developed quietly without opposition to Church officials, and the grass-root renewal they have produced has been, and continues to be, truly revolutionary.[28]

A basic ecclesial community is composed of about ten to a maximum of thirty Christians from varied walks of life. It is not a clique, but truly representative of the diversity of the Church. The members seek to deepen their shared faith, to live true community, to grow together in prayer and liturgy, and to organize themselves for outreach to others. Their life, made up of regular meetings for prayer, community, and planning, is a blend of spontaneity and simple structures that facilitate coresponsibility and significant roles for every member.

Like individuals, groups have their own life history and phases of psychological development. This movement through stages of growth is not possible in a parish because the parish is too large. But the basic ecclesial communities can identify their growth stages and deliberately move to a more mature group manifestation of their faith and Christian community life. In this way the small group satisfies the basic needs of individuals for liberation, social adaptation, fulfillment, and success. After all, people do not join any kind of group, including religious ones, unless they feel they will truly benefit and will obtain success in proportion to their efforts.

Basic ecclesial communities developed for two reasons: first, the lack of priests, with the resulting need for laity to organize themselves; and second, the dissatisfaction with large-scale parish life, often because of a desire to share faith more deeply with a smaller significant group. The basic ecclesial communities are having impact on the lifestyle of the Church and on the role of the priest. They are drawing young people into the life of the Church and deepening the quality of Christian sharing and faith. Pope John Paul II met with representatives of some of these communities and praised their life and vision.[29]

This phenomenon of laity forming ecclesial communities is an indication of the style of ecclesial life many of them want. These groups do not have the financial, communitarian, structural, or authority problems of the parish or diocese. They are free of the concerns that have accumulated around the management and business side of running the Church: personnel problems, overconcern with structures, careerism, and financial matters.

The basic ecclesial communities have in some way been more successful than the family, since they are based upon a deliberate choice and commitment made for religious development. Families are being challenged to renewal, the reintegration of faith into home life. It is generally easier to found than it is to reform, and this is one of the communities' advantages. They offer deep relationships, flexibility in structure, integration of each person into the common life, and significant outreach in daily life. They have an impact on the life of the universal Church and on civil society also.[30]

The Lay-Centered Foundational Church

It is important that we open up a dialogue and eventually integrate the revelation, vision, and teachings that come to us "from above" through a descending ecclesiology, with the insights, commitment, vision, and awareness that come "from below," from the foundational Churches. Otherwise our ecclesial vision will be weak and will tend to produce two Churches, not one. Signs of this nonintegration are everywhere in the Church today, as when we find ecclesiastically controlled ministries, prayer groups, and faith-sharing groups, and non-ecclesiastically controlled forms of the same commitments.

The following outstanding traits of life in the foundational Churches are already helping to build up the universal Church, and we must keep them in mind for future theology, pastoral planning, and spiritual life.

1. In local expressions of foundational Church, priests and religious are frequently absent because of their decreased numbers. Already in many parts of the world, the growth, development, and vitality of the Church are therefore most evident in lay groups. This is where the common identity of Christianity is often best expressed today. Furthermore, the ranks of committed laity will grow, and a wider, more pluralistic approach to Christian commitment will develop.
2. Many of the great issues of theological debate among clerics and theologians are simply of no importance to many participants of the local foundational Churches: canon law, celibacy of the priesthood, the extent of papal authority.
3. In foundational Churches we see a general upgrading of the image of all the baptized to a dignity which will not be laid aside when those groups enter the parish or diocesan structure.
4. In small faith groups, the members, whether priests, reli-

gious, or laity, experience new ways of living authority within the Church, and strongly claim their rights in civic life. These attitudes will transfer to the larger Church experience.
5. We witness simplification, decentralization, and broader ecclesial representation in the organization of cell Churches.
6. Professionalism in one's own career is expected, and this carries over into the ecclesial group. Evaluation is facilitated by spontaneous and positive criticism, and members elect each other to a wide range of community services. These developments will be more and more expected from the universal Church.
7. Extensive involvement of laity in the mission and ministry of the Church is seen in local Churches today. This involvement, rarely so extensive since New Testament times, is here to stay; those Churches will likely demand that they make direct contributions in policy and pastoral planning within the universal Church.
8. The primacy of religious leadership in these basic ecclesial communities is unquestionably with women. This will remain and grow. In our Church today, men are increasingly occupying managerial roles, and the women are emerging as the leaders.
9. In a rapidly changing future-shock world, decisions of conscience must be made rapidly and locally. With the decrease in numbers of priestly ministers, frequent recourse to authority figures, such as we have had in the past, will become difficult. As all the baptized are increasingly called to responsibility for faith, pastoral planning will need to make conscience formation a top priority so that local Church decisions will be genuinely Christian.

Lay Responsibility in the Local Church

Lay Responsibility for World Development

There are three aspects of the laity's responsibility in the local Church. First, their responsibility as Church to the world and its development through their daily work and socialization. Second, their responsibility to build the foundational Churches consisting of their own families or local groups. Third, their responsibility to bring their Christian commitment to the wider regional Churches of the parish, diocese, and universal Church. In each case, the responsibilities of laity are challenging to themselves and to the wider Church.

Carrying out one's responsibility for the development of the world is perhaps the greatest dimension of the layperson's life. This sense of commitment and faithfulness in the midst of distractions and discouragement is the basis of all spirit of mission in the Church (L 16:1) and is the principal form of lay mission (C 31:1). Simultaneously a believer and a citizen, each layperson tries to harmonize the two with the aid of a well-formed conscience (C 36:6; L 5:1).

At times, laypersons are powerless and are walked over by people who disregard them or oppose them; it is hard to persevere. In daily life, laity see the importance of competence and specialization, but they must also live with the need to give and take, to acknowledge the rights of others, to respect their freedom of conscience.

To survive in daily life, laity know they must change, be willing to experiment, and be open to explore new ways of interacting with friends, coworkers, superiors. Forced to live and struggle where things really matter, they see the secondary nature of ecclesiastical life and the overriding importance of their ordinary daily life. Not everything they do merits to be called "ministry," and they know it; nevertheless, they are immersed in the true mission of the Church: to serve and save the world.

As they face the daily crises of life, laity learn the need for conscience formation and see the value of a friend who will listen, give intellectual input, and share in reflection.

They live with the ups and downs of politics, experience that top administrators rarely affect one's daily life, learn to recognize service or control when they see it, and are beginning to see the impact of their organized actions.

Laity may need encouragement at times, but they live and struggle with the cross at every turning, for their lives are burdensome and sacrificial. There is a priestly dimension to the worker or the mother to which no ritual can compare.

To the parish and universal Church, laity bring this experience of faithfulness in the midst of hardships and distractions. They bring an awareness of the true values and mission of the Church. They have the healthy experience of competence and the appreciation of the importance of experimentation for survival. They can easily transfer to the Church their positive ecumenical experiences and their knowledge of the ups and downs of the political process. In short, laity's principal contribution is a sense of reality and perspective that can challenge ecclesiastical narcissism and the frequently overbearing dimension of religion, with its excessive laws, required rituals, and constant financial need.

Lay Responsibility in Foundational Churches

Although laity live in the midst of the world, the secular cannot define the layperson. Rather, being Church is the essential of a Christian personality. Vatican II stressed the laity's role in the world, and this is valid if being in the world is not made the exclusive defining characteristic. In fact, the central quality of the layperson is to be Church wherever he or she is.

Laity's first encounter with Church is in the foundational groups of family or basic ecclesial community, where they experience community and common mission. If their groups are intervocational, they will give a wonderful insight into Church. In every case, there will be lay leadership of one kind of another. Moreover, the leadership in foundational Churches is closely identified with the group and is not "out there" to be criticized. Leadership within foundational groups is generally, if not exclusively, collegial, and there develops a more realistic appreciation of the struggles of leadership.

Foundational groups are built through the pains and crises of community growth, and when some members leave, as is inevitable, the group learns the pain of separation. However, no foundational group can mature if the members compromise their positions, and so even opposition can be viewed as real friendship.

The whole process of building foundational Churches is itself the principal asceticism of Church life today, and the local Churches can call forth qualities and attitudes needed at every level of Church life. There is no basic community without a genuine sense of mutuality in service, love, and authority.

The foundational Churches also develop the practical dimensions of election of office holders, collegial government, effective subsidiarity, and thorough evaluation. If they have a priest, he can totally relinquish administration and concentrate on mediational ministry.

In their apostolic outreach to others, foundational Churches frequently work ecumenically. Moreover, in the daily struggles of local life, they get used to making rapid decisions and using provisional solutions. Foundational Churches react against passivity; they foster coresponsibility, a corporate sense of mission, and a commitment to genuine discernment.

These foundational Churches, then, can give an insight into what it means to live as Church today. Their appreciation of vocational gifts and their capitalizing on the charisms of everyone are rich dimensions of their ecclesial vision. Their approach to leadership is both healthy and creative, and foundational Churches show the variety and potential of lay leadership. The asceticism needed to build a foundational Church includes precisely those qualities necessary to build the kingdom today. The basic communities' approach to structures is also enlightening for the wider Church, which needs to learn better ways to live collegially, work professionally, and evaluate responsibly. Foundational Churches are especially valuable in fostering active involvement by all and a true sense of coresponsibility.

Lay Responsibility in the Parish, Diocese, and Universal Church

Laity come from their daily experience of the world and from their foundational Church to meet with other local Churches to celebrate together as a community of communities in the parish. The Vatican Council challenged laity to three areas of parish responsibility. First, it is the laity's responsibility to participate "knowingly, actively, and fruitfully" in the liturgical life of the parish (Lit 11). Second, with growing awareness of their baptismal responsibilities, laity make themselves into living communities (M 19). Third, they are called to a sense of coresponsibility for the Church, for they "have an active role to play in the whole life of the Church" (CT 43:7).

Turning to more practical details, the decree on laity specified that laity could show their spirit of coresponsibility by offering their special competencies to the parish and diocese, helping with the administration of Church property, and serving on various pastoral commissions and parochial and diocesan councils. Moreover, it is also part of lay responsibility to hand on catechetical instruction, work with converts, and at times take the place of the priest in his evangelizing ministry.[31]

From the experience of daily life, laity bring to the secondary groups of the Church an awareness of the importance of competence in themselves and in their ministers. In their foundational Churches they learn coresponsibility and bring that awareness to the parish or diocese even if it is possibly unwanted. Their experience is one of pluralism, and, painful though this always is, they can bring this perspective of struggle for broad acceptance to the possible divisions of parish and diocese. Laity are learning of their charisms and of their obligation to use them (C 33; L 3:3). They are becoming more aware of their unique gifts from the Spirit for the benefit of the Church. Furthermore, their experience of intervocational or team ministry in their local Church brings with it appreciation for others' vocations as well as for their own.

In post-Conciliar years, laity have seen much growth but have also had to feel rejection in the put-downs found in Church documents, the job losses in ministry, and the mere temporary toleration of their new roles.[32] This growth in spite of rejection is a way of living the spirituality of the rejected Jesus, and in the long run it will benefit the Church as a whole.

A dimension of the laity's ministry of evangelization is commitment to the study of theology. The Church desperately needs a spirituality of marriage, work, and leisure, to mention just three topics. While clergy and religious can help, the main creative work must come from laity. As numbers of clergy decrease and numbers of laity studying theology increase, we can anticipate that future directions in theology will be very different from those of the past.

At times, the topic of ecclesiastical authority seems all-absorbing, and discussion about it quickly becomes emotional. Laity can bring two healing dimensions to authority. First is the realistic judgment that authority is not so important after all. This does not imply a rejection of Church teaching but an identification of what is real and biblical as opposed to the accumulations of history. Second, laity can help purify ecclesiastical power and control when that power and control are simply mimicking or even going beyond the exaggerations of worldly leaders.

Closely connected with a more realistic and human approach to authority is the layperson's awareness of the narrow significance of Church laws. Far too much time, energy, and anxiety are given to promulgating laws, insisting on their observance, and spitefully punishing those who disregard them. Laity look on with shame and disgust and can challenge the Church to refocus its interests.

To their parishes and dioceses laity can bring a sense of competence and coresponsibility, an experience of pluralism, a willingness to grow through rejection, and an awareness of their own vocation and charisms. Their study of theology will give new directions for the future and call for a refocusing of authority and law.

The importance of the local Church today is giving more significant roles to laity. In their increased development of foundational

Churches, laity are surfacing as responsible leaders or collaborators and are stimulating an authentic lay voice in the Church. They bring their experience to the parish and diocesan Church, and their increased contributions are already producing and will continue to create new depths of Christian community.

Chapter 3

WORK

Introduction

The Vatican Council is the modern point of departure for revaluing the role of the layperson in the Church. The portrait of the layperson presented by the Council had developed slowly in the Church since the beginnings of the present century. Papal initiatives, especially those of Pius XI, and the insights of theologians like Marie-Dominique Chenu, Yves Congar, Karl Rahner, Edward Schillebeeckx, and Gustave Thils gradually prepared the Church for the new synthesis of Vatican II.[1] At the same time, the biblical, liturgical, ecumenical, and lay-apostolic movements were challenging all Christians to new attitudes and new levels of awareness in faith. Finally, local spiritual movements of prayer, social involvement, family life, and ministry were being enthusiastically welcomed by laity throughout the world.

However, this reassessment of the role of the layperson in the Church was complemented by a second development of incalculable importance for laity. This development, confirmed by Vatican II, was the theological appreciation of the intrinsic goodness and autonomy of the world.

In the centuries before Vatican II, it was common to distinguish between the religious and the secular spheres: the former was of value for afterlife, but the latter was not. Commitment to develop the temporal, or secular, sphere of life could become an "occasion" for religious merit by referring work in the temporal sphere to the glory of God, or by making a good intention to dedicate the work to some worthy cause. However, all activity in the temporal sphere was considered to be of no intrinsic value.

This negative evaluation of the world, and of all activity and work in the world, obviously had repercussions on the Church's interpretation of the mission of laity, since practically all their life was spent in interaction with the world. Matter, work, development, and progress were not thought to have religious significance. This world was understood to be passing away and to have nothing of lasting value except religious attitudes fostered in interaction with the world in work, study, research, social betterment, and business or political expertise.

Since the first decade of the present century, there have been studies on the theology of the world, matter, work, and progress. There have also been new studies on the relationship between the present and future life, in which absolute futurist eschatology gave place to salvation-history eschatology and proleptic or anticipatory eschatology. The former considered that work in this world was in itself of no value to the construction of the new world, whereas the latter saw that our work in the world developed into, or anticipated, the new world of the afterlife.[2] These two developments in theology and eschatology prepared the way for a reinterpretation of the value and dignity of human work and also outlined the possibilities for lay spirituality.

In this chapter we will focus on the laity's normal everyday world of work and reassess its human and religious value. We will hold that work is the laity's normal means of Christian growth, their spirituality is basically a spirituality of work, and their duty of interest in world development is actually intensified by the very fact of being Christian.

Approaches to Work: From Curse to Mission

Vatican II's Positive Approach to Work

Laity have suffered considerably from a negative interpretation of work based on the curse of Adam's efforts after the fall (Genesis 3:17–19), from the negative view of matter derived from dualistic philosophies (especially neo-platonism), from an exaggerated spiritualism associated with the development of monasticism, and from the equally imbalanced work ethic of the last century. All these unfortunate developments give rise to what Ed Marciniak calls "shoddy" or "misshapen theology."[3]

The Vatican Council saw the development of the world through work as part of the plan of God and intimately linked to Christian faith.[4] It emphasized that God is Creator, the ultimate source and end of all things,[5] and that he endowed creation with its own stability, laws, and intrinsic value. In fact, laity in their work should always be aware of God's directive presence (CT 36:3). In this vision of faith, we see God as having a definite interest in human effort, progress, and development (CT 36:3). His plan is that through their work men and women should control the earth, restore it, develop it, and bring it to perfection (CT 34:3; 57:2; L 7:1).

God's plan for world development through human work also included the great gift of liberty, the Council affirmed. This gift when misused brings sin, which can stunt God's plan. In fact, sin can radically change the context of world development, block human fulfillment, and result in disharmony between people and their world (CT 13:2, 4).

The consequences of sin, mentioned by the Council, are profound.[6] People are thwarted in their use of this world and fail to see any connection between their work and their faith. They feel a basic uncertainty regarding the direction to give to the world and how to organize their efforts. They lack balance in their decisions and can become blinded by materialism. In fact, as a result of sin "The world in which we live does not correspond to the state in which God willed and created it."[7] This situation does not diminish the dignity of human work, but it reminds Christians of their weakness.

Although infected by sin, the world of work is still intrinsically good. When the world stamps out Christianity, Christians *can* respond by stamping out the world. However, faith helps people see the true meaning and value of their efforts in relation to their final destiny (L 4:3). The world is good because it comes from God (CT

11:2, 36:2), is a sign of his enduring love (R 3; M 9:3) and a means of human growth and salvation (B 12:2).

It is because of this that the Church sees involvement in world development through work and technical progress as a prolonging of Christ's redemptive work (L 5:1). The Church is the sacrament of the world, committed to renew it (M 1:2). This mission of world development is carried on especially by laity in their daily work (C 31:2; L 22:1). As God's original creation was good, so too is the ongoing creative effort of the laity's daily work (CT 12:6).

Laity's Responsibility to Consecrate the World

Theological reflection and Church teaching in recent decades have not only emphasized the intrinsic goodness of the world of work but have also challenged laity to work in such a way that they show a true commitment to this world's development and progress. Although they interact with this world, use it, and enjoy its benefits, as Christians their work for world betterment is always detached, for their progress is not a primary end in itself, but only part of their journey to God. The Council calls laity to heal the world of sin, animate it with Christ's presence, transform it into what it is capable of being, dominate and control it for human advantage, and consecrate its development to Christ.

While flight from the sinful elements of the world will always be a part of the life of Christians, they have a fundamental commitment to develop the world through their work. Their efforts to improve this world are part of God's plan, are a clear sign of faith and dedication, and are in accord with their vocation to subdue the earth to the glory of God and to the advantage of humanity.[8] In doing so, laity better themselves in their labors and help others too (C 36:4).[9] They acknowledge the autonomy of the world and yet see its link with God.[10]

In the last analysis, the work of laity is part of their priestly responsibilities, and the Vatican Council included, for the first time in a major ecclesiastical document, the laity's consecration of the world as part of their priestly responsibility: "Thus, as worshippers whose every deed is holy, the laity consecrate the world itself to God" (C 34:2; M 41:6).

Work is not a curse but a call to construct a better world in union with the Creator.[11] Work is truly a mission, the normal means of Christian development (C 31:3; CT 76:6). It is the basic expression of human creativity and the normal way of humanity's self-realization (C 31:3). This work for world development is part of the Church's task. The success of the Church's mission often depends on laypersons' performance of their duties, even when they are unaware of the religious value of those duties (C 35:4).

In transforming the world, men and women transform themselves. There is a dynamic link between their work and their Christian growth. Faith clarifies the link between the two (C 48:3; CT 40:4; 41:4). Any split between "the faith which many profess and their daily lives" is roundly condemned, and neglect of daily duties is said to jeopardize salvation (CT 43:2-3). Rather, laity are called to "gather their humane, domestic, professional, social, and technical enterprises into one vital synthesis with religious values" (CT 43:3).

While all men and women may well expect one another to contribute to world betterment, the Council insists that Christians, because of their faith, are "more stringently bound" (CT 34:3) to work for a better world because in their efforts their faith can prove its fruitfulness (CT 21:6). Christians in their daily work need to be more conscientious (CT 43:1), responsible (M 36:2), and creative (CT 43:4). Their faith furnishes them with incentives to work well (CT 57:1). Their anticipation of God's final gift of a new earth "must not weaken but rather stimulate . . . . concern for cultivating this one" (CT 39:3). The task is gigantic, but on it Christians will be judged (CT 93:1).

The Church's theology and teachings have developed significantly since the times of a negative view of the world and work. Unfortunately, the integration is not complete, and frequently we still experience a departmentalization of life, with religion understood as something distinct from the daily life of work. Even the post-Conciliar emphasis on ecclesial ministries for laity has had the negative side effect of reducing the challenge to better the world through human labor. Many have lamented this.[12] However, recent understandings have challenged especially laity to a sense of responsibility for others and for the development of the world through their work.

The Dignity of Human Work

Work as a Christian Vocation

The seemingly ordinary conditions of laypersons' working life are very special. While involved in secular professions and occupations "from which the very web of their existence is woven" (C 31:3), laity sense that they are "destined for work and called to it."[13] They are called there so that being "led by the spirit of the gospel they can work for the sanctification of the world from within" (C 31:4). This awareness that it is ordinarily in daily labor that a person can "be a partner in the work of bringing God's creation to perfection" (CT 67:2) indicates the dignity of work.

Laity are on the border between the progress of technology and the relevance of religion. Excessive trust in technology and scientific progress, the fruits of human genius, can lead people away from religion to a presumed self-sufficiency and can make each of us a "stranger to things divine."[14] Christian vocation includes the difficult task of enthusiastically committing oneself to these two values, keeping them distinct, and yet appreciating how deeply they are connected.

In the daily labors of their working life, laity are in the center of the arena of where the Church needs to be. They are called there to be people of the Church at the heart of the world, so that in their worship they can be people of the world at the heart of the Church. The usual temptation for committed Christians is to center their lives more on Church issues, whereas the mission of the Church is to be in the world for the service of the world. This danger of misdirection of energies and of misunderstanding of vocation is quite real. "The greater involvement of the laity in Church-internal activities may itself reflect or result in an ecclesiastical narcissism and privatization of the laity themselves."[15] But most laity, because of their daily experiences, will always be broad in their interests and involvement.

Christian vocation cannot be defined by what someone does in his or her spare time. Consequently, volunteer work in the parish is not a person's vocation. Christian vocation cannot be described by specific jobs "which serve the institutional Church or generally help people. . . . The helping professions are not necessarily more appropriate for committed Christians."[16] Furthermore, Christian vocation cannot be defined by Christian attitudes or good intentions we have while working. "There are some jobs which cannot be done in that way, and there are some jobs which ought not to be done in that way."[17]

Christians' working conditions are also their divine mission. Laypersons in the context of their working day are the Church in the world and for the world. "Whether a job is merely tolerated, or is the joy of someone's life, it does have some relationship to a person's faith position."[18] A growing awareness that we are Church, and a deeper realization of the vocational and missionary qualities of ordinary work interact to help construct our Christian personality.

There is neither mention of nor need for Paul or for Aquila and his wife Priscilla to stop being tentmakers (Acts 18:1–3), for Lydia to stop being a merchant of purple material (Acts 16:14), for Cornelius to give up his command as a centurion (Acts 10:24–48), or for Sergius Paulus to abandon his work in government and politics (Acts 13:7–12). Christian calling does not imply abandoning responsibility for the world, but on the contrary committing oneself to it. Christians are called to work to better humanity. As Christians, their work is their very vocation. Through it they grow, help others, facilitate the welfare of humanity, and raise the world to a new level of existence.[19]

The Encyclical On Human Work

On September 14, 1981, Pope John Paul II published his third encyclical.[20] This pope has created for himself more opportunities for encounters with the laity of the world than any other pope in history. He has visited laity in their factories, civic centers, and government offices. He has shared their joy in their weddings, pride in their culture, satisfaction in their work. He has been immersed in the daily grind and joys of lay life. He knows firsthand the hardships of the factory, the exhilaration of sport, the intellectual challenge of university life, and the daily pressures of unjust government. In this third encyclical, he uses the occasion of the ninetieth anniversary of Leo XIII's *Rerum Novarum* to direct his pastoral concerns to the challenge of the world of work.

Three characteristics of work govern the flow of his teaching: the vocation to work is part of God's plan, work is a specifically human activity, and work always develops within the context of community. The interaction among these three components constitutes the very nature of Christian work.

This rethinking of the importance of work for Christianity comes at a very appropriate time. The context of daily work is vast, and technological progress and economic and political developments make major changes inevitable. However, it is not clear whether these changes will respect and enhance the dignity of workers or will lead to their exploitation and possible abandonment. Hence many questions and problems fill us with both hope and fear.

Since lay life and vocation are intimately connected with work, the Church tries to renew its teachings in light of changed modern conditions. As more and more jobs become computerized, types of work are different and therefore create new problems and pastoral concerns in such fields as nursing, medicine, and business ethics. We need to find new meaning for work, to integrate leisure into work, to educate to the use of free time, and to foster creativity in new kinds of work.

John Paul II locates his own encyclical not directly in papal teachings on work but in the tradition of papal interventions in social issues. For him the question of work is the key to the social question. If we are to make life more human for all, we must direct our concerns to the problem of the world of work.

The Bible, with its literary forms and styles of stories, teaches that God not only made work a necessary part of human life but also made it the occasion for people to cooperate with God and share in God's creative work. Salvation history consistently shows us two aspects of creation: the world is created for people, and people are given a mandate from God to develop the world.

Men and women fulfill their obedience to the Lord's mandate through their work. However, with technological developments, fewer and fewer people are working, and machines are supplanting their former masters. Industrialization, telecommunication, miniaturization, and computerization are the allies of the worker, making work less burdensome, time-consuming, and boring. However, while technology produces economic progress, it also gives rise to personal ethical and socio-ethical questions that individuals, corporations and nations will need to face. The new relationship of the worker to these developments needs to be established, because work is an essential characteristic of humanity and an essential dimension of Christian vocation.

Human work is a sharing in the creative work of God. It is intended to be a mission and an experience of profound dignity. Moreover, it is *work*, not just some *kinds* of work, that is noble. Some societies have viewed levels of work as menial and others as better. John Paul refers to the "gospel of work" that shows how the value of work is not determined by what is done but by who is doing it. Work's *prime* value has nothing to do with what is being done; its value lies in the human dignity and Christian vocation being realized in the work. This position excludes neither the practical need for different sorts of work, and different remunerations for work, nor the need to seek improvement and promotion in work. It does identify priorities and gives a context in which kinds of work, remuneration, improvement and promotion can be judged.

The "gospel of work" is the basis for evaluating development in the world of work. Christianity brings a new way of thinking, judging, and acting about work and a unique way of viewing the worker. A particular threat to the right order of values comes from interpretations that see workers merely as means of production or labor forces, or their work as merchandise to be bought or discarded. In each case workers are treated as objects, and their human call and Christian vocation in work are reduced to insignificance. Such violations of their dignity tend to unite the workers against the oppressors. Rather, workers are themselves the principal purpose of the whole process of production.

Work is part of the basis of human dignity. God's plan that people subdue the earth through their labor and personally grow in doing so remains unchanged. Admittedly, work is hard, but the struggle brings satisfaction and other benefits, such as a sense of achievement, health through exercise, an awareness of being needed, and so on. Work is good for us all, as we realize even more in times of high unemployment. The struggles of work also foster virtues of industriousness and creativity and make us more aware of injustice as we struggle against it ourselves. Even the helplessness experienced in difficult work can make us humble.

Like everything good, though, work can be used to exploit, punish, oppress, and degrade. Accordingly, the pope pleads for a return to the personal dignity and valuing of the worker.

Work leads to personal growth and to social benefits for our civic communities. It is also intimately connected with the development of the family and the nation. Work sustains a family, and a family is the training ground for correct attitudes to work. The same is true of society in general. Work is a major support of society, for it helps create its culture and its standard of life. Society can be the educator of the people to correct approaches to their work.

Work in Perspective: Leisure

The Pursuit of Leisure

In 1967 Americans spent over $70 billion on leisure activities; in 1977 the amount had more than doubled to $160 billion; and in 1978 the trend continued as the figure rose to $180 billion. By the early '80s we were spending over $200 billion a year, and the amount has continued to increase. Not only do we spend enormous amounts of money on leisure activities, but we also have the time to enjoy them. We have longer vacations than ever, longer weekends, shorter working hours. If all vacation time were added together, the average American could have a nine-day vacation every two months. In addition to this, a greater percentage of citizens consists of older, retired people whose whole life can be nonwork. Many people are retiring earlier, and married couples often take one job between them. Those who can choose among job opportunities take into account the quality of life offered in a given area and will accept less salary in exchange for an environment that provides for better use of leisure.[21]

Our parents and grandparents worked to exist. Their lives were built around work, and their spirituality came out of a work ethic that emphasized devotion to work well done. How many of these people—laity but priests and religious, too, of a similar age—are lost when the work ends! Yet today many people of all ages work so they can have leisure. They now have two lives: a working life and a leisure life, and the latter is the more important. For them, as for the ancient Greeks and Romans, what is important is leisure *(schole, otium)*; work is simply not-leisure *(ascholia, negotium)*.

In recent years we have continued to hear of the "Relaxation Response," "Cue-Controlled Relaxation," calisthenics in large factories, Transcendental Meditation, yoga, and so on. All indicate a conviction that much disease is dis-ease—a lack of leisure. Psychologists who have tried to sketch for us the integrated person have shown a consensus in emphasizing the component of leisure. Some sociologists have suggested that this lack of true leisure is a basic mistake at the center of our culture, and that unless it is corrected the wasteland will never end.

The importance of the leisure component of life is clearly seen today in lifestyles, personal values, economics, and health concerns. It is stressed by quality-of-life groups, psychologists, and sociologists. But where are the theologians? A few prophetic warnings have been given, but theologians generally have not yet taken the challenge fully into account.[22] The results for Christianity in general and for our approach to work in particular are devastating, because we cannot achieve an adequate theological base for Christian life today without considering leisure. "The scant attention which theologians have paid to the understanding of leisure has contributed in no small measure to our incomplete theology of other aspects of Christian living."[23] This is true especially of our approach to work. I am not suggesting that we make yet another addition to the thematic spirituality of the last decade. Rather, a leisure component should be integrated into every aspect of Christian life and should complement our work.

The Relationship Between Leisure and Work

The various understandings of leisure presented in writings of recent years indicate three basic interpretations. The first sees a close relationship between leisure, free time, and relaxation. In the past, leisure was the prerogative of the rich who did not need to work. With industrialization and eventually a decrease in working hours, almost all individuals began to enjoy some leisure time. In fact, our modern society has made leisure accessible to more people than ever before. Unfortunately, for many, the increase in nonworking hours has led to a fruitless mimicking of a previous leisured class. "Free time" has become a measure of social and economic well-being and can result in empty idleness or be filled with unproductive activities and quantities of so-called leisure goods. Americans have access to entertainment, sports, weekends away, prepackaged trips and vacations, and these pastimes require equipment—motor homes, cabins, clothes, TV, and so on. For many, leisure is no more than this consumption of non-work-related goods, and the opportunity to relax. This interpretation, which I suspect is the most common in the U.S. today, confuses the real pleasures of leisure with spending on objects of leisure. This confusion about the real meaning of leisure makes many turn leisure into work.

This understanding of leisure contains some positive insights. It emphasizes the close relationship between work and leisure. It claims that the latter can be fully enjoyed only by one who also works. It stresses that there must be a balance between work and leisure, or a personal stunting will result. That leisure in the widest sense includes ease, rest, and amusement and that it is not merely the idleness and boredom of free time are also asserted in this understanding. But this notion either sees leisure as passivity or injects into free time the same attitudes required in work. There is no real change or rest. People who are competitive in work are competitive in their leisure sports, in their acquisition of leisure goods, and in the social image they portray. All this is work and achievement. It is not an integration of work and leisure but a prolongation of working attitudes into free time.

A second general understanding identifiable in several writings, particularly of the last decade, is the equation of leisure with creative self-development. Leisure is not simply freedom from work and obligations; such "leisure" can result in boredom, killing time, or filling time. Rather, leisure is freedom for growth, openness to one's inner self and capacities. It is an opportunity to pause and appreciate the wonders of the world around us and to grow as human beings in the process. Through creative involvement in "the things I'd love to do if only I had the time," it develops a wellspring of self-identity outside of one's job. It is an occasion to share while free of tension, an opportunity for exercise, fun, and release, a time to stretch interests and revitalize senses. Leisure is the enjoyment of the natural ecstasies of life, such as travel, nature, friendship, the arts.[24] It is a time for fantasy and festivity.[25] "At a time when work tends to depersonalize and submerge people in anonymity, leisure will 'restore the balance and given an opportunity for the individual initiative, self-assertion, and self-expression that will enable a man to discover himself as a person.'"[26]

This second understanding of leisure is, I believe, accurate but incomplete. It certainly corrects the negative, passive, and at times stunting elements in the first understanding. In fact, this second one not only refuses to equate leisure and free time but even requires that we give up free time to creative leisure, to genuine recreation. It emphasizes the truth that personal development depends on the intregration of work and leisure and that it is the latter that leads to quality growth. Work contributes but only in so far as it is "an outpouring of the spirit," in which case it presupposes leisure. Work and leisure go together.

In this view, leisure gives opportunity to develop some of our God-given creative qualities.[27] The repetition of work does not accomplish this, but the self-discovery and self-development of leisure can. What is learned in the creative effort of leisure can then be integrated into work.

Work and Leisure Seen in Faith

The second understanding implies a commitment to growth and indicates the potential value of leisure in Christian growth. Further reflection, however, suggests a third understanding, one that stresses a close connection between leisure and faith. Our notion of leisure depends on our notion of the human person. For a believer, a humanistic approach to life is not enough to ensure the fruits of leisure. Rather, the integral human development that results from leisure must naturally include the religious. In the appreciative wonder of a restful enjoyment of the universe, the believer is open to the divine. In fact, "it is in leisure that a person grows ripe for encounter with God."[28] Experience confirms that we are better able to express our faith through prayer and worship in periods of leisure, when we are relaxed, able to concentrate, and quiet, and receptive. Leisure is also necessary to experience many of the truths we say we believe in: God in our heart, the Lord in community, and the beauty of God's creation. Furthermore, leisure is necessary to nourish our faith: savoring a joy or sorrow helps us savor God; concentrating on a beautiful scene helps us concentrate on God; listening to friends helps us listen to God.

Let us reflect for a few moments on our faith and leisure's connection with it. God has always called us, as in the Sabbath commandment, to celebrate joyfully and thankfully what he has given us. We are called to pause and publicly acknowledge that life is a gift. Does our life indicate that we believe this? Unlike those who profess some other religions, we Christians claim to believe that God is near to us, in us, in others, in the wonders of the world. In leisure, away from the distractions of work, we have time to appreciate the presence of God and to cultivate attitudes necessary to meet him: receptivity, wonder, stillness, and silence. We also believe we can experience God individually and in community, but does our life show this to others? Are we "working" tourists who look at everything and see nothing, or do we pause, appreciate, wonder, and praise God who, we believe, reveals himself in creation? We do not earn salvation by our work; leisure helps us appreciate that it is gift. Leisure is the corrective that puts work in perspective and shows forth our faith.

A distinctive characteristic of Christianity is that its revelation is principally a person, Jesus Christ, rather than a mere listing of teachings. When we look at this person who is the content of our faith, we see him walking through the grain fields, fishing, camping, at meals with friends, taking a retreat by the seacoast, emphasizing the beauty of flowers, enjoying a wedding, entertaining his friends by cooking their meal. He has no permanent job, nor does he minister in working situations. He calls people in the leisure circumstances of life, and those who do not appreciate his call are the ones who have eyes but cannot see, ears but cannot hear because they have grown dull (Mk. 8:18). Others are described as unwilling to participate joyfully in a banquet because they have working reasons to be elsewhere (Lk. 14:15–24). Jesus assures those who answer his call, "Come to me, all you who labor and are heavy laden, and I will give you rest" (Mt. 11:28).

Genuine leisure culminates in the religious. In fact, when it runs its course, it ends liturgically in the praise of God.[29] Work never follows that path unless it is undertaken in a leisurely manner.

I am aware that I have not given a detailed explanation of leisure but have only hinted at what constitutes it. A leisured approach to life will be different for each person. It is certainly not merely free time, although that is necessary. In fact, a person can have a leisured approach to his or her work. Leisure is more an attitudinal approach to life than the amount of "free time" a person has. When leisure and work complement each other, they enrich each other and lead to integrated living.

Work in a Lay-Centered Church

Lay Responsibility in Work

Every person is privileged to bear personal responsibility for self, others, and the world. The context where laity exercise this is principally in their working lives. Here they are called to use all their talents, their self-trained consciences, and their skilled judgment. In work, men and women must increasingly act on their own initiative and judgment regarding the human and Christian value of decisions at work. The immediacy of decision making at work demands maturity of conscience, courage to make rapid decisions, humility to live with mistakes, and trust enough not to become discouraged. Workers reflect the Creator not only in their products but also in their need to judge individual and communal actions.

The demands of work today force people into very delicate situations with difficult ethical and socio-ethical consequences. Workers who wish to be Christian must educate themselves or gather with others for formation in decision making. For instance, those work-

64 / LAITY'S MISSION IN THE LOCAL CHURCH

ing with the elderly or in Hospice work with the dying need special support and formation opportunities, but so do those in business enterprises, as many "corporate classrooms" seem to indicate. One's personality is formed at work; unless people are responsible and aware of their Christian mission, their work will form them into non-Christians.

The lay-centered Church leads to a world-centered Christianity rather than to a Church-based Christianity. For decades, Christians have emphasized the Sunday Church celebration as the main religious experience of the week, and then extended its beneficial effects to the rest of the week. Now, however, with the responsible commitment of laity, we are looking toward a Christianity experienced and celebrated in the working world of Monday through Friday, and extending its beneficial effects into the Sunday liturgy. This blending of Christianity and daily working life is of significance in evangelization, for it relates the news of salvation to all of life rather than to a minor segment of it.

This lay responsibility to build a world-centered Christianity also includes the prophetic mission of social reform. Often the world of work is characterized by less-than-Christian values, and workers individually or as groups need to prophetically challenge such injustices as degrading working conditions, faulty products, poor-quality work, mismanagement of the firm, or waste of other people's money.

However, prophets not only speak words of challenge; they also call for vision. Workers can exercise a visionary role in calling for change in management structures, in seeing new and better ways of production, in complementing work with leisure, in establishing a dimension of social responsibility in their places of work, in supporting others who suffer the insecurity caused by change, in calling for long-term goals in business rather then the short-term quick gains so characteristic of recent years.

It is also a prophetical mission to portray Christian values by the quality of one's life. It is in their working life that laity carry out part of their baptismal responsibility and are "witnesses," "powerful heralds of faith," and "perform eminently valuable work on behalf of bringing the gospel to the world" (C35).

Part of lay responsibility in work is to use well the political and economic power of work. Our nations and churches contribute much good to our individual and social lives. However, they are also made up of power blocks with their vested interests, and it is the general rule that both national and Church governments ignore the desires of large numbers of the people they claim to serve. Vatican II gave some good advice when it said, "Citizens . . . should be on guard against granting government too much authority" (CT 75:3). Laity should insist on genuine participation in all forms of government and should contribute to structural reforms that facilitate collegial government. At times, laity will need to be nonconformists, dissenters, or critics in order to be truly loyal to the organizations of which they are part.

There needs to be some counterbalance to the powerblocks of national, ecclesiastical, or business managements, and responsible Christian workers should pursue goals in this direction. Pope John Paul II's support for Solidarity is well known, and he has also spoken to his own Vatican employees on the advantages of workers' associations.[30]

In the arduous tasks of daily work and through the tensions so frequently associated with work today, laity are responsible above all for a mission of service. Their work is a service to themselves, to their families, their employer, the city, nation, and beyond. Needless to say, poor work becomes an equally extensive disservice.

Work is also an occasion for service to one's fellow workers in the example one gives, the values one stands for, the support and outreach made, and the sense of community one builds up. So many individual and social needs can be satisfied for oneself and others at work that it is a situation of remarkable potential for good.

Christian workers can serve others by helping them appreciate that life has a meaning and is not over at death. They can witness to Christianity's defense of the dignity of the human person, of freedom of conscience, of the goodness of the world, of the rights of men and women. Christian laity can proclaim the importance of a sense of duty, of good and responsible work, of the need to share and participate, of the necessity of genuine leisure, of the goodness of culture (CT 40-44).

Work as a Major Component of Spirituality

Our commitment to work is a specifying feature of our Christian personality. If work and spirituality are separated, the resulting tension hinders progress and mature living. Life proves itself Christian in the happenings of one's working life, where holiness is characterized by a sense of baptismal responsibility and vocation, an awareness that life is grace, a commitment to evangelical life, and an openness to new priorities.[31] God cannot be loved in opposition to our daily working life, nor apart from it, but only served in it. In their work laity use their talents, show their virtues, and prove their fidelity.

Laity are close to God in their work, as they share in the Lord's creative activity, continue it, and even advance it (CT 34). Work is the laity's participation in the servant-kingly function of Jesus (C 36). Christianity's vision of work is both elevating and humbling at the same time, for it shows both our mission and our distance from accomplishing it.

Jesus himself was a man of work, a craftsman like Joseph, and a model for us all. He spoke constantly of the world of work, especially in his parables. His disciples were involved in all aspects of work and challenged Christians to follow their example responsibly (1 Thess. 4:11; 1 Pet. 4:10; 2 Thess. 3:10-12). Genuine individual and world progress are directly connected with a spirituality of work.[32]

In work, laity experience the cross of Jesus. Their endurance and voluntary acceptance of the hardships of work, their reaction to the temptations to sin that come in times of work, and their struggle-filled efforts to build good relationships at work are their "sufferings of the present time" (Rom. 8:18), their daily living of the cross of the Lord. Fidelity to Christian values is more severely tested at work than in any other normal time of each day, and yet here the Christian layperson is generally alone in his or her profession of faith.

In their work, Christians can become focal points of a real presence of Christian values that can also be a sign of hope in the new and better life that lies ahead, as they contribute to constructing a better world, taking risks, and exploring new possibilities for improving their work, their services, their working conditions, and their contributions to society.

It is especially in work that Christians can develop through their courtesy and love a genuine spirit of dialogue and collaboration. This spirit is the basis for Christian love and compassion that are so profoundly needed in our burdened world.

Work highlights mission for laity. The world they interact with and develop is good in itself, and their work has a value in itself. Laity are called to consecrate the world to the Lord, and their dedication to better that world through their work is incumbent on them more than on anyone else, specifically because they are Christian. In our own time, we have seen a deep appreciation of the dignity of human work and of laity's vocation in work. However, to be a constructive contribution to the world, work must be complemented by the ease, rest, reflection, and joy of leisure. As we move from a Church-based Christianity to a lay-centered Church, we emphasize more the laity's mission in work and their spirituality of work. They become again the biblical sages who provide the bridge between the Church and its mission to the world.[33]

Chapter 4

FAMILY

Introduction

Most of the Church's teachings on family have been handed down by people who have never started a family of their own, who were taken away from their family at an early age, and whose access to their family was strictly controlled. Most of the Church's teachings on sexuality have been presented by celibates who have never expressed sexual love in intercourse, whose early life and training often looked down on affection even toward their own relatives, and whose theological roots were frequently tainted with a dualism that despised the physical. Most of the Church's teachings on parenting and education have come from people who had no children of their own, who were protected from the daily hardships of family life, and who had no direct responsibility for someone else's life and maturing.

The help, guidance, and support given to families by dedicated priests and religious have certainly been worthwhile in many ways. Their sensitivity and compassion, understanding, and insight have contributed enormously to the development of family life. Furthermore, their detachment and celibate commitment have given them a balance and corrective to extremes of passion and selfishness. However, this pastoral sensitivity has generally been exercised within the perimeters of teachings that came from Church officials. It goes without saying that celibate ecclesiastics or religious can give valuable guidance and teachings to married people and vice versa. But what simply boggles the mind is the quantity of official interventions and teachings on family formulated by celibate bureaucrats who rarely if ever have sought input from married people. The inevitable consequences of this kind of inadequate pastoral practice remain with us: the image of family presumed by Church administrators corresponds very little with Christian family life in the real world.

Generous attempts to help family redevelopment have been made by many bishops, priests, and religious in the years since the Vatican Council in personal advice, family counseling, and the direction of spiritual movements of family development. Even the Synod on the Family, held in Rome in 1980, and the preparations for it and the resulting Apostolic Exhortation on the Family were serious attempts to focus on the centrality of the family for the future growth of the Church. Unfortunately, most of these attempts, and certainly the synod and its document, have failed, principally because of a lack of significant lay participation.

The development of Christian family life depends on the input of married laity. They must develop for themselves a theology and spirituality of the family. As people of the Church, they of course need to be open to the insights and challenges of Church management personnel and dedicated religious. But the basic synthesis or syntheses in the area of family life do not come from these two minority groups but from married people themselves.

In this chapter we focus on the importance of the family as the foundation of the Church. We then consider sexual love, responsible parenting, and conscience formation. Finally, we consider the responsibilities of laity in this family dimension of the lay-centered Church.

Family as Foundational Church

Changes in Family Life

Organizing one's family as a genuine expression of Christianity is more difficult than it used to be. The economic pressures of modern life frequently necessitate that both husband and wife work, and this leads to new needs in the use of time for themselves and for their children. The financial insecurity that many couples face is potentially closer to gospel poverty than is the lifestyle of many religious. However, the anxiety often becomes oppressive as couples realize that they are the only generation in recent times that are not financially better off than their parents.

In the first decade of this century, the average length of a marriage was between eleven and twelve years, and parents would rarely live long after the last child had left home. With the advancement of medicine, the couples typically live much longer than their predecessors, can expect that practically all their children will live to adulthood, and can anticipate at least twenty years of life together after their last child has left home.

Within families the various roles are very different from what they used to be. Women are now independent, with their own job, career, and identity. They have clear goals of their own as well as shared family goals. In fact, the wife may well be the main breadwinner of the family, the manager of family affairs, and the real leader of family development. The husband has needed to adjust his own role as a result of the positive development in the social status of his wife. He has needed to look seriously at his own contribution to the family's life and has been challenged to find creative new ways of self-development and of integrating his own and his wife's growth. Finally, the increased education of children, their earlier sexual development, and their delayed psychological development have resulted in new crises and challenges for everyone in the family.

The development of family life can even be victimized by statistics about itself. It is oppressive to keep hearing about broken marriages, the increased divorce rate, separations, annulments, and family violence. It creates the image of a life choice destined to failure, with the resulting feeling that if you do fail, it is not all that serious, because everyone else is failing too.

In addition to recent economic, social, and statistical pressures on family life, there are a series of positive trends that are part of a changed approach to family life.[1] The reverse side of the problem of new roles is the growing recognition of the full humanity of each family member. Some people are marrying younger and assuming personal responsibility, a few women have equal opportunity and salary, many other women have increased family responsibilities, and children have a recognized independence and a life of their own.

Although contemporary families face many problems, they often take a more mature approach to the problems, and passage through problems and difficulties can lead to mutual growth and development. Many couples, accepting their own family background, environment, and education, move with this acceptance toward new levels of growth.

Amidst the recent negative statistics, there is a growing conscious valuing of family life. Couples know they are going to have to work at family development. Many of them are more aware that long-term happiness comes with the integrated development of family values and requires conscious commitment and deliberate effort. Dialogue, communication, responsibility, decision making, collaboration, and planning are part of a family's growth.

Furthermore, recent theology, spiritual movements, and parish renewal have stressed the religious importance of family. The growing realization that baptismal commitment is lived in the context of a home, not primarily of a church, has heightened the significance of family life.

There is even a growing appreciation of the value of the family's contribution to human development. The disruption of civic and social life caused by the breakup of marriages, the fighting over custody of children, and increased numbers of runaways, to mention just a few problems, has challenged all to appreciate the civic and social value of healthy family life. Increased sexual immorality and perversion, despite their evident and direct evil effects on society, dramatize the need for reconstructing Christian family values.

As the pressures and challenges of family life increase, networking and peer support have also increased. These forms of family ministry have led to enriching interaction.

There is no uniform way of looking at family life. Recent trends, whether negative or positive, affect families in different ways and degrees. Not only are major ecclesiastical documents too general to be relevant, but so too are most syntheses, whether from sociology, psychology, or spirituality. Family life is as varied as couples are. That is why the responsibility for development lies at the basic level of foundational Church.

Family as Domestic Church

In Chapter 2, when discussing local Church, we concluded that the foundational expression of ecclesial life was the family. Family is not only the fundamental cell of social life but is created in the image and likeness of the loving Trinitarian God. God in innermost mystery is not a solitary being but a family, and human beings are made in this image and likeness, called into existence through love and for love.[2] The family finds its identity and mission in God, to be a community of life and love. Its identity and mission are stressed in Christianity through the vocational sacrament of matrimony in which the couple becomes the Church in miniature, a small-scale Church, a domestic Church.

If the universal Church is to be a sacrament of unity for the world and a prophetical, priestly, and servant Church, it can be so only if families live in Christian union and exercise their prophetical, priestly, and servant ministries. If the domestic Church is not strong, the universal Church has lost the living stones out of which it is built, and it remains permanently stunted.

Married Christians have always known that their main Christian responsibilities are in the family and that the quality of their religious life depends upon the quality of their family life. The concept of being a domestic Church was sensed by Christians before it was reproclaimed by the official Church. It is equally true that Christians have realized that extra activities in the local parish do not substitute for a lack of commitment at home and can never bring peace or satisfaction when the latter is lacking. The growth of Christian life depends primarily and foundationally on the family.

Although clergy and religious may present their own vocations as states of perfection and may have their views supported by official teachings,[3] married laity have the nagging feeling that the state that has greatest potential for a more perfect realization of Christian life is actually the family. It is not necessary to do anything extra or to "churchify" or sacralize life. Rather, the domestic Church *is* the prime way of spiritual growth. Husband and wife are gifts to each other. Dedicated to each other's growth, they are channels of God's love to each other and are called to share their faith in their home life.

While the importance of family has been both sensed by married laity and taught by the Church, the recent changes in family life have brought new crises and have challenged laity to reinterpret Christianity in the new circumstances. The decreased importance of parish life, with its broad range of devotions, has in many cases not been replaced by a spirituality of the domestic Church. It is crucial that married laity fill this vacuum with a new spirituality that comes out of their own faith and condition.[4]

Family is domestic Church, the Church in miniature, the most basic manifestation of Church life. It is created in the likeness of God, blessed as a sacrament, and seen as the primary sign to non-Christians of the embodiment of Christ's teachings. Within the daily experiences of family, married laity have the most effective means of evangelization, and the future of the Church will depend on how they use them.

Sexual Love and Life

Sexuality and Intimacy

Because of our lengthened life span, most Christian marriages now last four times longer than they did at the turn of the century. Such lengthy marriages never existed before,[5] and they also demand more from the partners than in previous generations. Moreover, while we hear a lot of negative criticism about the failure of marriages, people today probably work at their marriages more than previous generations did. If marriages are to survive the extended length and greater challenges of today, sexual intimacy needs to be well developed.

Intimacy includes companionship, affection, harmony of mind, and daily mutual support. It leads to mutual effort to bring about any needed cultural, psychological, or social renewal of married life in order to facilitate the increased dignity and mutual growth of the partners. Intimacy involves the good of the whole person, enriches all expressions of body and mind, and is manifested in many ways. It is the art of daily loving another and requires discipline, concentration, patience, thoughtfulness, concern, and a sense of humor. It is shown, experienced, and fostered particularly through the phsycial expressions of sexual love in tenderness, a passion for each other, and physical union. Sexual union in intercourse is the sign, expression, and pledge of the total union of husband and wife. It constitutes the outward sign of the essence of the marriage commitment and makes present what it symbolizes and expresses.

Husband and wife are ministers to each other both in the sacrament that binds them together and in the ongoing life that results from the sacrament. Sexual intimacy and the physical gestures that manifest and foster it require balance between concern for self and concern for another, between faith and trust in another and the need to take risks. They require skill and practice in order to bring joy, pleasure, and ecstasy to another and to oneself in another.

Married love is a sacrament. Admittedly it was not until relatively late in the Church's history that it was declared a sacrament; it is only from about the twelfth century that the Church explicitly refers to the sacrament of matrimony.[6] This recognition of the vocation of the couple does not of course diminish the autonomy or intrinsic goodness of the human expressions of married life.[7] Those expressions are healed and perfected by the Lord's redemption, become part of a Christian life and vocation, and foster the life of intimacy. Furthermore, sexual love, to be genuinely Christian, requires an attitude of permanent commitment and faithfulness.

Obstacles to Overcome

No other area of moral theology shows such discrepancy between official Church teaching and the practice of Christians as does that of sexual morality. Theological and secular journals and newspapers frequently give statistics on Catholics' approach to divorce, abortion, premarital sex, homosexuality, and contraception. The last issue shows the greatest gap, with over eighty-five percent of Catholics practicing contraception.[8] It would be superficial and inaccurate to suggest that the reason is a growing selfishness among married Christians. Selfishness is not so much the answer to lay reactions as it is to the actions of ecclesiastics who control lay input into Church teaching on family. However, there does seem to be an extraordinary distrust of Church officials in areas of marriage and sexuality.

Perhaps one reason for this is that Church involvement in matters of sexual morality has historically been rather negative. Although St. Paul speaks of the redemption *of* the body, attitudes have frequently indicated that people thought he meant redemption *from* the body! Some early Church Fathers were too influenced by the dualistic tendencies in neo-platonism and tended to judge negatively matter and the physical aspects of life. These positions were heightened by monasticism's emphasis on virginity and the consequent despising of sex.[9]

The history of Christian spirituality has not prepared us for a positive approach to conjugal life. While the Church did condemn as heretical movements that rejected the sexual expressions of life, it nevertheless remained tainted with dualism and consistently advised flight from the world, hatred of the body, self-denial in sex, and temporary abstinence. In fact, marriage was seen as "a remedy for concupiscence." The approach to priestly celibacy is fundamentally and historically a put-down of the sexual life of the married, and the suggestion that celibacy is a more perfect state in life seems to be yet another negative approach to sexual life.

A further obstacle to the development of sexual life is the sinful selfishness of immature personalities that leads to pseudo-love that disintegrates one's commitment. It is almost impossible, at the time, to distinguish between selfishness and altruism in the physical manifestations of love. Often, people are blinded and influenced by unconscious attitudes and desires. Perhaps the only way to ensure selflessness in sexual intimacy is to consistently develop it in all other aspects of one's married life.

In the pressured circumstances of today, a problem for sexual intimacy is often the fact that spouses do not know each other as they ought. Frequently, both spouses have jobs, take on overtime, belong to health or sports clubs, and watch a lot of television. The lack of quality time given to each other produces a situation where it becomes impossible to meet each other's expectations for intimacy.

There are, then, serious obstacles to the growth of sexual love. Among them are unbalanced Church teachings, the negative approach of spirituality, personal selfishness, and social pressures of modern life.

Sexual Love and the Church

The Church's mission from the Lord essentially consists in witnessing to love. Vatican II spoke of the Church as a sacrament of unity, a sign of the union and love God brings to the world. Jesus reminded us many times that we will be judged on love.

Sexual love is not only the physical expressions of love but a total way of life that includes every dimension of the couple's relationship. It is a sacrament of love in which the spouses commit themselves to the essence of Christianity, the pursuit of love. Their sacramental commitment is not only a sign and witness to love but an effective presence of love in the Church. Married laity can call the Church back to love and intimacy. At the same time, laity in striving for love can be witnesses both to religious and to the world that seems to have lost the love it so desperately needs. In fact, the family has the mission of showing the Church and the world what true love is.[10]

As part of this ecclesial witness to love, married laity are called to heal love and integrate sex and eroticism into their Christian life. True love at times will manifest itself in sexual union and at times in abstinence. Lovers know the value of abstinence as a sign of affection and true love when a partner is unwell, worried, or not desirous of union. Thus, spouses integrate elements of the evangelical counsel of chastity into their lives too. To abstain from physical union in order to show love needs sensitivity, control, and a contemplative dimension to one's loving.

A further contribution to the Church from the sexual love of married Christians is the way they accept and live out equality between the sexes. Many Christians cannot understand Church administrators' inability to treat women fairly and justly, and they challenge the Church's discriminatory practices by bringing to their married life a simple objectivity in which the woman is neither treated unjustly nor put on a pedestal in what is nothing more than a more subtle put-down. And on the broader level of role assignments, married couples who have lived through changes in relationships and roles can help the Church deal with them too.

Finally, married couples can assist the Church by developing a family spirituality. They know what is conducive to growth and fulfillment and what is harmful. They can identify the broad outlines of an asceticism of married life, the main lines of a theology of conjugal love and life, and the correctives to previous exaggerated emphasis on sin and law.

The joy and love of married life is a sign of the kingdom, an expression and a form of Church life, and a persuasive witness to the world.[11]

Parenting and Family Education

Creating a Christian Environment in the Home

We grow and develop as Christians not in our spare time, nor during an hour on Sunday mornings, but in the way we interact and live during the prime periods of our life. We have already seen that work is one of these commitments; the other is the family. It is part of parents' baptismal responsibilities to create a Christian family atmosphere. In fact, this is the prime ministry of parents, a ministry of unique importance for both the Church and civic society.[12]

Before creating a family atmosphere conducive to the education and formation of children, husbands and wives need to create a Christian atmosphere that facilitates their own mutual growth. Channels of God's love to each other, they should not resign themselves to a "reduced ideal" of their life together[13] but should also commit themselves to a sharing in faith. This will imply practical efforts to organize their home in such a way that they give time to reflection, prayer, discussion, and celebration. This first level of evangelization is the essential one; all others are extensions of this.

The begetting of children, as a fruitful expression of love, leads to a new home environment. The responsibilities to educate children are one of the first ways the Church experiences the nature of authority. The exercise of authority can be violent or redemptive, dictatorial or evocative, used for control or used for service.[14] The family environment shapes not only the personalities that make it up but also interactions in the wider communities of civic and ecclesiastical life. Christian parents quickly see that authority is mutual and shared. Each member—husband, wife, or child—calls the others to growth, change and development. They influence each other's behavior through constant motivation and challenge. In helping children discover their unique individualities, parents actually discover something of themselves.[15]

This mutual education includes the responsibility to be informed, the wisdom to judge, and the willingness to accept the pain of growth. It implies mutual respect, a willingness to struggle for consensus, and an openness to the Spirit in every family member. No matter how dedicated the parents are, or how cooperative the children are, there are always the painful experiences of differences of opinion, of dissent, and of those who choose to go their own way. The divisiveness that every family faces can harden people, lead to autocratic attitudes, and end in un-Christian polarization. But modern parents and children are learning to grieve over their family's differences, live with positions they never thought they would have to live with, and accept differences while trying to maintain the essentials of their love.

The family environment is the first and principal school for the members. For the first time in centuries, parents now send their children to Catholic schools whose teachers may well know less than the parents and be less educated than the parents. Likewise, some pastors may know less about contemporary religion than parents do. The family is a school of holiness, social development, ministry, moral development, and deeper humanity.[16] It is in the home environment that family members build up their own spiritual life with the daily hardships and sacrifices that come with family life. Very few religious communities or priests' groups need to face daily struggles like those of family development. It is a state in life and a way of holiness through which the Church is truly blessed.[17]

The home environment leads to the fruitfulness of parenting and facilitates the fulfillment of the obligations of parents to develop the Christian dimensions of their family life. A Christian environment facilitates a sharing of faith, a Christian exercise of authority, an appreciation of mutuality and mutual dependence. It is an experience of the cross, a school of life and Christian values, and a way of holiness.

Family Ministries

Christian families, like the first disciples of Jesus, are sent out in twos on the mission of the Church. This implies the couple's shared expression of the threefold ministry of Jesus: priestly, prophetical, and servant.[18] These three functions are lived out in the many forms of family ministries.

The prime family ministry, as we have seen, is to witness to the Christian quality of family life. This witnessing by the cultivation of Christian attitudes has positive influence on other families, local society, and even the state, nation, and international sphere. It implies not only the integration of positive Christian attitudes and practices, but also the social ministry of publicly defending Christian family values and prophetically challenging society's disregard of them. This social ministry extends to challenging unjust conditions in other families and the lack of respect for the dignity of the family or of life generally.

Family ministry is a ministry of education by example. This is part of the parents' evangelizing responsibilities: to bring the gospel to each other and to their children by the Christian quality of their lives. Their ministry of education will include pre-marriage preparation of their children, guidance in their early years of married life, and help during the time of parenting.[19]

With the decreased numbers of priests and religious, parents need to assume more and more of the religious education of their families. This is desirable, since the parents are influential and effective. However, this requires serious study including Scripture, theology, and social doctrine, and it is matured through education for critical thinking and mature evaluation of religion in general and Church practices in particular. Their own ministry and that of their children can be maximized by a thorough and diversified formation in religious education.

The educational responsibilities of family ministry include preparing children for Church ministry. Families that are truly alive with the spirit of service foster such service in their children. Furthermore, this commitment to ministry will be a healthy base out of which full-time ministry—whether lay, religious, or priestly—will develop.

The family is a ministering community to its own members by the quality of its life. However, we need a ministry that will develop Christian life in other families, help hurting families, cooperate with single-parent families, and contribute to the Christian growth of the separated and divorced.

The essential family ministries are internal to the domestic

Church. While it is not necessary or even desirable to go out night after night to work in the local parish, the family should make sure that its ministry has an outreach dimension to it. Nowadays, when economic conditions often force both parents to work, or force one of them to take two jobs, people have less and less time to give to voluntary Church work for others. When possible, however, some outreach in service to the larger Church or civic community is a desirable dimension of family ministry.

Since work is one of the two basic areas in which our spirituality develops, it is a major family ministry to painstakingly prepare children for a Christian approach to work. This will imply education in skill development, conscience formation, participatory government, professional responsibility, and interpersonal relationships.

Among the many family ministries is the service value to others of developing a joyful and happy family life that others can see, yearn for, and strive for. This can include the sharing in family groups where all can learn from the strengths and weaknesses of each other's family life.

A further ministry is the fostering of all kinds of family prayer. Quality family life is not likely to survive on the Sunday service alone, and parents will need to take seriously their responsibilities to grow personally in prayer, train each other and their children to pray, and together prepare for the community worship of the parish liturgy.

Part of Christian parenting and education is the commitment to ministry and the responsibility to facilitate ministry in one's children. One's approach to ministry is a good indicator of one's commitment to be a genuine domestic Church.

The Importance to the Family of Conscience Formation

The Nature of Conscience According to Vatican II

Christians are baptized into a freedom so extensive that it is conditioned only by the demands of love for God and others. This freedom, which is a part of Christianity, does not lead to selfishness; rather, it is a freedom for service of Christ and of others in Christ. The demands that Christ and others in Christ make on us are dictated to us not by laws, for we are free of the law (Rom. 8:21; 1 Cor. 9:21; 1 Tim. 1:9), but by the internal, personal judgment of a Spirit-guided mature Christian—in short, by conscience (Jn. 8:32; 1 Cor. 6:3). Love is the driving force in our lives (2 Cor. 5:14; CT 19:1), and its demands are so clear that it becomes a rule of life (CT 16:1). This Spirit-guided rule of life is not a rule imposed on a person. It is a rule of life, a spiritual law in each one's heart (CT 16). We continually see that this personal judgment regarding how we are to use our liberty and personally direct our lives is being conditioned by love. Conscience leads Christians to act with the dynamic, active love of Christ and to do those personal, fully conscious and free acts that are of decisive significance both in the Church and in the salvation of others.

People of the present day make much of their rights to free decisions and self-direction of life, and they should (CT 17:1; RF 3:3). This obviously does not mean that Christians are exempt from the requirements of law (CT 41:7). However, it is true that each Christian, in dialogue with God, is responsible for the personal direction of life (RF 3:3). Conscience is a synthesis of risk and humility. It is a sign of spiritual and religious maturity (RF 3:4).

Christ communicates his will to us, but the final decision on the carrying out of his will comes from a spiritual action so individual, internal, and personal as to be no longer Christ's but one's own. This judgment is the Christians' norm of living and is effective in every aspect of their lives. This conscience-judgment is so personal, universally applicable, and of such leavening value as to be equated at times by St. Paul to faith itself. On the full and complete living of what this judgment directs, Christians will themselves be judged.

There will frequently be tensions, and sometimes errors in decisions, but a well-formed conscience will always summon one to love good and avoid evil. To ignore its urgings in preference to someone else's views is both immature and blameworthy.

Conscience is the prime rule of our moral life. Moreover, we are not referring to a true conscience formed by the Church but simply to conscience (CT 16:2; 79:2). The former restricted interpretation was excluded by Vatican II, whose final document on religious liberty stressed the freedom of the act of Christian faith and respect for conscience even when it errs.

The exercise of conscience is not only a right but an obligation. Christians are called to take responsibility for directing their own lives and to follow honestly the judgments of their own consciences. In times past, because of their lack of education, Christians relied on others, particularly the pastor, to make moral decisions for them. But this undesirable luxury has ended, and each one must now live by fidelity to his or her own conscience. The crucial ethical issues that affect our daily lives are focused particularly in the family, and it is there that fidelity to conscience must be rooted.

The Family's Exercise of Conscience

In a time like ours, when attitudes and structures are changing, Christians must learn to form for themselves right and true judgments of conscience based on the sources of faith and the moral norms of personal Christian convictions. In exercising conscience one reflects the power of God, for conscience shows the Godlike qualities of freedom, creativity, and judgment.

Conscience is not something we already fully possess, but something we are constantly growing into. As circumstances change, conscience must evaluate differently and at times arrive at different conclusions. However, each one is responsible for the formation of his or her conscience.

The first component of a mature conscience is self-evaluation, which means that Christians, looking back over their lives, analyze how they have often reacted. Possibly some combinations of circumstances blind correct judgment or stunt a Christian evaluation of events or circumstances. However, self-evaluation can teach us a lot that can encourage us and help us assess future situations.

To be reliable, the exercise of conscience should be part of a prayerful life, for prayerful reflection and sacramental life are the normal prerequisites for the guidance of the Holy Spirit. People who rarely pray cannot be assured that their conscience is accurate, and though conscience should be respected even when it errs, the evaluation that conscience judged erroneously should lead to changes in one's self-evaluation.

The prudent exercise of conscience should be influenced by the consensus of the faithful on matters of teachings and morality, for Christian belief includes the conviction that the Holy Spirit guides the people when they universally agree on an aspect of daily life.

For people of faith, the exercise of conscience depends on a knowledge of the sources of faith, especially Scripture and the universal teachings of the Church. None of these sources, neither Scripture nor Church teachings, must be interpreted literally, and so conscience must also be based on consensus of interpretation among theologians and scholars.

However, decision making nowadays is even more difficult than formerly. We live in a future-shock society where the changes of every five to ten years are equivalent to the previous changes of an entire generation. In times past, one could consult an authority figure such as a pastor for decisions on difficult faith or moral issues. But changes in business practice, politics, social development, finance, medical practice, and sexual issues are so rapid, and the line between what is ethical and what is unethical is so difficult to identify, that pastors or religious figures are no longer the experts they used to be. Nowadays, they need to specialize in pastoral practice and are becoming more pastoral technicians than knowledgeable theologians or ethicists. Moreover, even when an expert can be found, there is often no time to consult him or her, for decisions must be made, and made rapidly.

Conscience is exercised locally by individuals or small groups of Christians, a practice intensified by the absence or unavailability of experts. As always, they will need to make decisions and take risks.

And they will need the maturity to react against discouragement when their family support group discerns they were wrong in their decisions.

The formation and exercise of conscience will primarily occur, then, in the local Church. However, local domestic Churches that take conscience formation seriously will of course be open to input from the conscience of the broader ecclesial and civil communities. The exercise of conscience will become more necessary but more difficult in the years ahead. While conscience formation will be done in local family Churches, their members will need to identify consensus among the teachers, thinkers, and doers of the Church. Husbands and wives will need to do this for each other and for their children.

Family Responsibilities in a Lay-Centered Church

Responsibilities of Married Laity

There are signs that we are at the end of an era. We have empty rectories, priestless Sundays, and a growing irrelevance of international religious leadership. The pulse of Christianity is now more and more felt in local foundational Churches, especially families. As married laity come to the fore to develop the main lines of their own Christian identity, we hope it will be done with a true spirit of dialogue and benevolence, rather than with a mere reversal of roles and a grasping of control and power.

As the laity awaken in our time to the central importance of the family, they are becoming ever more aware of their baptismal responsibility. They see that the Church will not be built up except by the family, by responsible Christian mothers and fathers. In such conditions, they will need to be at the center of the dialogue between the Church and the world, will need to be aware of the broad societal changes in family life, and will need to understand deeply the Christian values of family life.

Previous generations looked to the Church's many priests and religious for leadership. This is fortunately no longer possible; fortunately, because the passivity of the laity is not a desirable feature of Christianity. The circumstances of this generation call for the individual commitment of every baptized Christian to assume responsibility for faith. This personal commitment is primarily focused on the Christian qualities and characteristics lived out in family life.

It is the responsibility of married laity to contribute their own experience to the Church's teachings on family, sexuality, and parenting. Moreover, since the Church is built on the strength of foundational Churches, one of which is the family, married laity's experience of building family life can help the wider Church communities.[20] With the commitment of married laity, which we are increasingly seeing, we are ready for the development of a theology and spirituality of marriage.

Married laity can enthusiastically develop a real sense of vocation, not only in service to each other and to their children but also to the whole Church. Their experience and understanding of married life are a theological source from which the Church can draw and learn.[21] Their sexual sharing and experience can be the prime guide for Church teachings in ethics and even ecclesiology. They can witness to the broader Church and bring a sense of affection, intimacy, and love to a Church more frequently identified with legalism, power, and control. Part of this vocation will include speaking out on theological and moral positions, even when it implies a clear non-acceptance of Church laws. This is necessary if the Church is to arrive at genuinely Christian conclusions. Teachings must be the fruit of reflection on the insights of those who build up the home environment of the domestic Church and formulate an effective family spirituality.

Married laity have a serious responsibility to minister to others, especially other families in poverty, sickness, weakness, and loneliness.[22] Family ministries must also be creative in reaching out to help solve the social problems of our day—for instance, in responding to the needs of adoption, hospitality for strangers, guidance to adolescents, formation of engaged couples in preparation for marriage, and support for families in crisis (L 11).

A further dimension of family ministry is the support that married couples can offer to priests and religious as increasing numbers of them struggle with relationships of affection and intimacy.

In short, then, in their daily working life, laity have responsibilities to organizations that make very rapid decisions. They also have responsibilities to the Church that fittingly makes decisions very slowly. The laity are at the cutting edge of Church and world. They do not have the luxury of a slowly changing Church administration, and they often do not share the values of a rapidly changing society. Rather, they walk the knife-edge between the two, bringing the concerns of each to the other. In this context, married laity have the serious responsibility to form their family conscience so that they can make decisions in light of their lived Christian faith.

The Prophetical Role of the Family

Secondary structures, such as the parish and diocese, are built on the primary foundational Churches, notably families. The Church of the future will increasingly resemble the families of today. If the latter are loving, open, sharing, ministering, prayerful, and prophetical, the larger Church will be too. For better or for worse, the family is the future of the Church. This is not to deny the radicalness of the grace of the Lord in history or in other expressions of Christian life, but it does presume that the Lord generally works through the channels of creation.

Moreover, development of family life will be the most effective way to acknowledge, both in theory and in practice, the central place of the laity of the Church. Individual laity, married or single, who are drawn into the official life of the Church frequently become merely new rungs on the hierarchical ladder and even manifest characteristics of clericalism rather than being an authentic lay presence. Lay integration is most effective at the level of families that become local domestic Churches.

The prophetical role of families includes the experiences of new, undefined models of the Church. Their own family life brings a new sense of community, a new coresponsibility, and a new incarnation of ministry. In fact, not only is the family a domestic Church, but the Church is also a family.[23] Moreover, the Church as sacrament of the world achieves its mission of witnessing to the world principally through family life.

Over recent decades, the structure of family life has changed. The equality and mutuality of spouses and the more rapid independence of children have led to new relationships and structures in families. This can be beneficial to the manaagement personnel of the Church, who need to face up to the desirability of changed structures that show greater appreciation of women and treat all persons responsibly.

The family can also be prophetical in living its social responsibilities. In fact, the teachings of the Church on social justice remain largely ineffectual without the responsible commitment of the family. A family's commitment to simplicity of life and a sharing with the poor can speak much more forcefully than the witness of priests or religious. For the latter, it is always difficult for people to distinguish between personal poverty and institutional wealth, and even when priests or religious live simply, neighbors continue to identify them with their wealthy churches or institutions. Nowadays, the public witness to evangelical simplicity and poverty is more clearly appreciated in family life, where the witness is corporate, long range, and lived in insecurity.

Family life has the potential of developing a broad and realistic spirituality. Husband and wife need to develop strategies for growth in their Christian commitment. In fact, at times there is mutual spiritual direction in morality, prayer, education, social involvement, and spirituality. This kind of mutual direction avoids some of the undesirable features of traditional forms of spiritual direction such as dependence, immaturity, male dominance, and self-styled gurus.

Family calls for mutuality of relationships and the creation of an environment conducive to the growth of the members. In fact, the family is committed to discover the originality of each spouse or child and to work for the development of the full potential of all its members. Family implies a commitment to love over an extended period of time. It demands a daily consistent witnessing to Christian values. These values must become the fabric of every day. Living with someone for a long time challenges to consistency of Christian response. By contrast, priests and religious can often move away from failures and try out another group. At times, they can be dedicated with some people and escape from others to solitude. But husbands and wives must be consistent and maintain their best for their families, or the families will challenge them.

A further dimension of the prophetical quality of family relationships is that the commitment of husband and wife is long-term—the only truly permanent and unbreakable commitment in the Church. The priest can be dispensed from his ministry and minister in another way and marry; the religious can be dispensed from his or her commitment and make other commitments and marry; but a married couple may not terminate their commitment and be married again. Family life calls people to the permanence of love, and as such it is the clearest revelation to the world of God's saving love for all. In the lay-centered Church, family life is the mainstay of the Church, its greatest embodiment, and its most effective means of outreach.

Christian families are the basic cells of Church life. The quality of their own family life, their ministries of developing a Christian environment in their homes, of parenting, and of education, and their educational service to both Church and civil society through conscience formation, give Christian families the opportunity to have a major positive influence on modern life. The responsibilities of family life train the members in a spirit of coresponsibility that also benefits the local and universal Church.

Chapter 5

OUTREACH IN SERVICE AND SOCIAL INVOLVEMENT

Introduction

The Old Testament prophets consistently rejected any approach to religion that neglected responsibility for social justice. The New Testament writers confirmed this emphasis and related it to the essence of Christianity, as for example Matthew in his presentation of the last judgment scene (Mt. 25:31–46). Since the beginnings of the twentieth century, both papal and episcopal teachings and the insights of spiritual movements have further stressed the need for integrating social commitment into any healthy approach to Christianity.

St. Paul, surrounded by an unjust world very similar to our own, reminds Christians of all eras that they should make the most of the times they live in "because the days are evil" (Eph. 5:16). Unfortunately, today's injustices are frequently so deeply rooted in cultural and political rationalizations that even Christians often consider them acceptable. Thus we are given plausible reasons for the differences between the rich and poor nations, and even hear religiously supported arguments for the subordination of women. Disorder is difficult to see when it is the usual order of the day. The great social encyclicals of this century, from *The Workers' Charter* of Leo XIII to *On Human Work* of John Paul II, have largely fallen on deaf ears, and the challenges of local ecclesiastical, religious, or lay groups have often been conveniently swept under the rug. Some Christians, seeking only the comfort of religion, have even opposed the efforts of bishops to arouse the baptized to a social consciousness befitting Christianity, as we saw in reactions to the U.S. bishops' 1983 pastoral on war and peace. Some Christian organizations and countries have committed themselves so much to power, control, and profit that their religion is dying from their greed. On the international scene we have Catholic leaders in some Latin American countries and elsewhere who deliberately maintain systems of injustice, and on the U.S. national scene we have political lobbies and political action committees with religious affiliations dedicated to maintaining the unjust status quo.

Christians have had little international impact on the growing selfishness of humankind, and even locally it has been a difficult task to call the baptized to outreach in service to others. Many complacent Christians will not sacrifice their social status and will consistently push aside the uncomfortable social teachings of this century.

Yet it is impossible to define Christians without reference to their responsibilities toward others. In our present situation our faith needs to prove its fruitfulness by penetrating our entire lives, including the social and political dimensions (CT 21:6; L 31) and by increased lived awareness of our responsibility toward others and toward history (CT 55). Non-Christians will measure the genuineness of Christians' commitment by their contributions to a rebirth of social justice.

At the local level of the Church, there are some positive signs of small-scale involvement in issues of social justice. Many parishes have programs to help the needy; ecumenical groups are organized to help the unemployed; and various Christian groups dedicate time and money to help street people, the homeless, and the hungry. Grass-roots movements have focused attention and raised the consciousness of Christians. Some pastoral leaders have proclaimed the need for conversion in matters of social and political justice.

Before the end of this century, Catholic laity will need to commit themselves vigorously to the irresistible requirement of social and political involvement as a means to direct our history and prove the authenticity of their religious commitment. It is here where the lay-centered Church needs to be seen in all its life-giving challenge.

In this chapter we will examine developments in the social teachings of Christianity and identify the importance of local lay involvement. In a world that seems incapable of breaking out of the vicious cycle of injustice, we will examine the alternative world vision that Christianity offers. Finally, we will look at the close link between social commitment and the credibility of Christianity.

Christianity and Social Consciousness

Recent Papal Social Teaching

For almost a century, the Catholic Church has forcefully challenged all the baptized to dedicate themselves to alleviating the miseries and sufferings of the world.[1] Seeing the concentration of wealth in the hands of a greedy few who controlled production and maintained inhuman working conditions for the poor, Leo XIII proclaimed *The Workers' Charter,* which called for justice between owner and worker, the right to private property, the desirability of trade associations, and the need for restrictions regarding accumulation and use of goods. Forty years later, at the time of Pius XI, workers were still treated unjustly, paid poorly, and deprived of any participation in the ownership of the firms they worked for. Wealth was still concentrated in the dictatorial control of a few. In that context, Pius XI called for a new social order in which competition would be controlled by government, and criteria would be established for wages. In addition, he recommended worker involvement in ownership and management, and even state ownership in some cases. He urged the wealthy to share their superfluous goods and to work for a more just distribution of wealth.

Although Pius XI had already referred to the need for international cooperation, John XXIII addressed the international dimensions of the social problem more fully. He taught that all private, state, and international ventures should always be conditioned by the common good and that the governments of his time were inadequate to promote the universal good of people. He responded to the social problems of his day by stressing the need for a strong Christian social conscience, the importance of human dignity, the advisability of employee participation in the firm and in profit sharing, and the necessity of safeguarding against the trend to monopolize. At the same time, under the threat of nuclear war, he urged concrete efforts toward peace, recommended the support of international authorities, and pleaded for disarmament.

During the reign of John XXIII, the Church celebrated the second Vatican Council. It was solemnly closed by John's successor, Paul VI, but before the closure, the participants promulgated the Pastoral Constitution on *The Church in the Modern World*. This document condemned the growing economic inequalities of the world, whether between individuals or nations, rejected the arms buildup and the lack of international accord, and highlighted the interrelationship between world peace and concrete solutions to the social problem. The Council appealed to all peoples to find new forms of international trade, urged corporate effort to arrive at economic and political decisions worthy of human dignity, and proclaimed to all Christians their responsibilities for the promotion of a better world.

In 1967, Paul VI yet again confronted the great social problems and, faced with a world that seemed to be committed to an unacceptable set of values, prophetically denounced the glorification of profit, competition, free trade, and private ownership, insisting that all these values are subordinate to social justice, world development, and the needs of others. He called for broader education, shared responsibilities, pluralism of professional organizations and trade unions, and even the expropriation of land if necessary for the common good. At the same time he challenged individuals to personal conversion, to an awareness of their own infidelities, injustices, and lack of involvement in constructive change.[2]

John Paul II's contribution to the resolution of social injustices focuses on the condition of human work and the concrete local context where social inequality originates. The basic outline of his teaching was presented in Chapter 3 of this book.

In the course of a century, Christian commitment to work for social justice has been progressively seen as a corporal work of mercy, a sign of true charity, a matter of justice, a component of peace, an integral dimension of world development, a participation in liberation, and a concrete living of the compassionate care of God, who is rich in mercy. At the same time, the responsibility for the resolution of social injustices and inequalities has been assigned to the teaching Church, to national governments, to international organizations, and finally to each individual worker in the concrete situations of each day. A commitment to outreach in liberational service is part of the very essence of being Christian, and it is integral to the daily life of every baptized Christian. Each must think in a new way, live a new social responsibility, and foster a new consciousness. For laity to absent themselves from the central social questions of today would be a damning form of infidelity to Christianity's social obligations.

Christian Motives for Social Responsibility

This has been a century of unparalleled challenge to Christians to commit themselves to social involvement leading to reform and the upbuilding of a just society. Social responsibility is integral to Christian life. It is rooted in the grace-filled call of the compassionate God, in our awareness of the pervasiveness of sin, in the belief we share in the redemptive incarnation of the Lord, and in our common vocational ministry to heal and to renew the world.

First of all, Christians believe in a generous, loving, impartial, and compassionate God who directs the unfolding of history. The development of history manifests human acceptance or rejection of the compassionate involvement of God. Therefore, "It is not ridiculous to hold oneself responsible before Society, the World, Mankind, History, or to write those words with capital initials—they designate so many faces of God, since they represent so many orders of his will."[3]

Men and women are made in the image and likeness of the compassionate God and must reflect his love in their lives in order to realize their own potential (1 Jn. 4:7; CT 24:3). It is part of our very nature that we are called to share the love of God with everyone. Christianity affirms that love of God and neighbor are inseparable (Mt. 22:37–40; 25:31–46) and that all religious observance without love is meaningless (1 Cor. 13:1–13).

Christians also believe that God is not only their source but also their end. They are pilgrims, and they never absolutize the world and its goods, but use them with detachment. This detachment, however, does not diminish their involvement but brings perspective amidst temporary joys, and optimism amidst the oppression and pains of life. With a sense of urgency, Christians strive to set up a world based on the loving compassion and justice of God (M 19;2). Hardness of heart and insensitivity, oppression of the poor and weak are the very opposite of Christian values.

Secondly, Christian teaching also focuses on social responsibility by its constant challenge to uproot the pervasive influence of sin. Attachment to wealth and power has always been forcefully condemned (Jas. 5:1–6; 1 Tim. 6:8–10; Mk. 8:36). However, today's world of abundance for some, false values, and un-Christian formulas for happiness leads to inequalities that offend the very nature of the Good News. Men and women today seem more preoccupied than they used to be with wealth, power, and the need for new experiences. This restless desire to accumulate and to experience is satisfied at the cost of the necessities of life for others. If the Christian image of God calls for a compassionate sharing with all, then a Christian analysis of today's world identifies the pervasive presence of new inducements to sin that exclude concern for others and abuse others in order to accumulate possessions and pleasures for oneself. The compulsive accumulation in modern society and its selfish clinging to what others need cannot be overcome without genuine conversion and the aid of grace (CT 25:3).

Scandalous inequalities in wealth and opportunity have been condemned by the Church for a century, but even many Christians do not respond to the conversional call because, like the rich young man in Luke's gospel, they are well off (Lk. 18:18–25). Sin is not only present in the compulsions of modern society but also in the omissions and neglect of Christians. The positive value of evangelical poverty is a Christian revelation that is grasped only slowly and at times reluctantly. It is urgent that Christians face squarely their individual and societal sin in order to overcome their pangs of conscience and in order to live up to others' expectations of them.

A third motive that Christians have for social involvement is the redemptive incarnation of the Lord. Not only is this the clear sign of God's love for all, but it is also the way of God's love. Jesus has irrevocably established the redemptive value of incarnation. Christians are now called to incarnate the compassionate love of God in their own societies (C 38; CT 40:3). Their incarnational presence can be educational, compassionate, healing, liberational, and even contestational. It is a critical insertion that leads to redemptive changes. The renewal of the world begun by Jesus (C 48:4; CT 58:4) is continued by the whole people of God, who now "do their utmost to alleviate the sufferings of the modern age" (CT 88:3). Christians in the concrete circumstances of their lives become advocates for values of justice. Faith spurs them on to seek ways of incarnating God's love for the benefit of all (CT 93:1). In fact, a commitment to perfect the work of justice is a consequence of faith (CT 72:2).

A fourth motive for social responsibility is the belief that in baptism we share a common vocational ministry to heal and renew the world. A life of loving service to carry others' burdens is an essential component of baptismal living (Gal. 6:2; Rom. 13:8; 1 Tim. 1:5; Col. 3:14; Jas. 2:15–16). It proves the genuineness of faith (CT 21:6) and is a vivid expression of God's providential care.

This responsibility for social justice will imply taking a stand, being in opposition, highlighting disagreement, and being ready for confrontation. Although previous generations of Christians fled the world, our generation must heal and renew it. This implies collaboration in economic affairs and social life, commitment to all forms of cultural development, involvement in human rights issues, and a dedication to political action. Christian social responsibility challenges to unity, justice, and mutual respect; it breaks down divisions, calls for openness, creativity, and change; it challenges to both individual and institutional conversion; it brings theological and religious convictions to bear on the theories and practices of economic, political, and social life.

Social Service: A Critical Ministry Today

Early Christians quickly appreciated that social service was an essential dimension of response to the Lord. They showed this in concrete ways in the early Church, but today we live in very different conditions that are so complex they require consolidated community responses. This is a vital area that is generating new forms of ministry, especially lay ministry.

St. Paul, in his final speech to the Church of Ephesus, gives us the only saying of Jesus recorded in the Acts: "There is more happiness in giving than receiving" (Acts 20:35). Early Churches had taught that the spiritual blessing of faith challenged Christians to share their material blessings with those in need (*Didache* 4:8; *Letter of Barnabas* 19:8). In fact, Luke claims that early Christianity is seen to be the community of God foretold by Moses (Deuteronomy 15:4) by the very fact that no one was left in need (Acts 4:34).[4]

Christians must be alert to others' needs locally and globally. Lack of concern for others manifests a religious selfishness contrary to Christianity's community commitment and service of others. Baptism includes a ministry of outreach to the needy,[5] in which both oneself and one's possessions are at the service of others (CT 69:1).

This service to others in need is carried out in social and cultural conditions that are profoundly different from what they used to be. We see this when we become aware of injustices throughout the world, such as regional and local hunger rarely experienced before, national poverty, and degrading unemployment. Nowadays, Christian ministry of social involvement requires broad community commitment rather than delegation of the huge task to a committed few. It implies a baptismal witnessing to social consciousness, volunteer work for the needy, and professional dedication.

A ministry of social service is best achieved by Christian communities rather than by individuals, for it is a work that requires integrating many charisms. Some in the Church listen to the world locally and internationally in order to discern genuine need. Others are political observers committed to an intelligent analysis of society; they can interpret the cries, longings, and aspirations of men and women. Others prophetically challenge and contest society's unjust values, oppose today's false prophets of social change, speak out for the oppressed, and denounce the oppressors. Still others are catalysts of change through their own work and through facilitating the involvement of others in social reform. Healthy Christian communities, then, become ministering communities that discern need, analyze the political scene, prophetically challenge, and creatively lead to new alternatives in social development.

Christianity's growing social consciousness and its increased commitment to social service are the most vital areas of ministry for the Church today. As we reflect on the new ministries of social concern, we can also see that these are areas of ministry that are most fruitful for theological reflection. In fact, all understandings of the term *ministry* are exemplified in social service: full-time ministers who are hired and directed by ecclesiastical government, part-time ministers (whether paid or volunteer), and all the baptized who are spurred on by a general spirit of ministry to the needy. At a time when we need to clarify the concept of ministry, Christian commitment in social involvement may offer an opportunity to do so gradually. Social services also make it clear that the sacramental model of ministry is inadequate, reserved as it is to the few churchgoers who are frequently quite well-off and not interested in, or are even threatened by, the Church's challenge to social involvement.

Social service is an area with many new practical options for ministry, and it is contributing to an expanded notion of ministry.[6] At times even responses to the same need are varied, and disagreement develops among those involved. Both this experience of pluralism and of disagreement in response are healthy signs of a mature Church. It also exemplifies regional variations in ministry, as each local Church responds to its community's most pressing needs.

Christian social involvement is the area of ministry that has the greatest potential for upgrading the service of laity. It is both the sphere of greatest practical relevancy in ministry for people today and the type of ministry best achieved by a lay-centered Church.

The service to social justice is the clearest example of a ministry that calls for creative leadership in facilitating new expressions of itself. It is in the whole context of social service that Church leadership can develop new ministries, call forth laity to ministry, show its commitment to involve others, and portray the vitality of the Church.

Finally, Christian commitment to social justice keeps believers' attention focused on the world and on the Church's primary mission of service to the world. This is a healthy corrective in times of excessive interest in internal Church life and ministries. The need to be committed to social ministries also reminds us that concern with the decreased numbers of clergy does nothing to solve the major weaknesses of Christianity. It would be more valuable to capitalize on the ministries of a lay-centered Church.

Service and Social Involvement

Lay Ministry to the World

Outreach in service and social involvement is essentially lay ministry. Although theologians and pastoral experts interpret the life and role of the laity in different ways,[7] there is a consensus that ministry to the world is the specific responsibility of laity. "The great forces that shape the world—politics, the mass media, science, technology, culture, education, industry and work—are precisely the areas where lay people are especially competent to exercise their mission."[8] John Paul II speaks of the laity as "the most immediate protagonists" of the renewal of the world, whose mission it is to evangelize and transform society and to be "participants in the entire reality of the world."[9]

Ministries of social involvement and justice are the special areas of lay responsibility (C 31:3; 34:2; CT 38:4). These ministries are not delegated to laity by the hierarchy but are essentially lay and result from baptismal commitment. Moreover, since the work of justice embodies the major concerns of people today, the upgrading of the image of laity is a direct result of the Church's commitment to social justice, for laity are precisely the Christians who carry out this commitment.

While outreach in service results from the world vision of Christianity, involvement is generally local. Some of the general principles of Christian social consciousness are presented by international Church leaders, as we have seen, but the concrete commitment is embodied locally in the specific circumstances of lay life. In the local Church, with a sense of collaboration and shared responsibility, laity create specific ministries to incarnate the general vision of the universal Church in such areas as family life, work, and politics.

All Christians share in Christ's priestly, prophetic, and servant functions, but it is the laity who in a particular way live out the servant qualities of Christ (C 36). In fact, the Vatican Council continually places the priestly and prophetic functions in relationship with Christ's service to the world. In order to be faithful to Christ's mission to the world, the Church must rely on the laity, who are well versed in the trends and needs of the world (CT 44:4; L 2:3; M 15:8).

The fact that the Church is the sacrament of the world means that one's condition in life is one's mission and that laity, who are immersed in temporal affairs of every kind, are called to see this as a mission that the Church can never be without. Laity's outreach in service is a proper, necessary, and distinct mission of specific value. It is so intimately connected with their own personal Christian growth that the latter is unobtainable without it. This sense of responsibility for the world is a major component of Christian faith.[10] Today we are challenged to face up to the problems of nuclear war, hunger, medical care for the elderly, dignity of and respect for the handicapped, women's issues, the changing face of poverty, and the need for political involvement. Living at the center of world activities, laity integrate their worldly vocation with their baptismal responsibilities, knowing that as believers they are "more stringently bound" to work for the welfare of others (CT 34:3). In fact, "faith needs to prove its fruitfulness by penetrating the believer's entire life, including its worldly dimensions, and by activating him toward justice and love, especially regarding the needy" (CT 21:6). Laity are called to have a lively awareness of their responsibility to the world, to unhesitatingly devise new enterprises to better the world, and to appreciate their special vocation in the political community.[11]

Ministry to the world is achieved, then, through laity. They live in the midst of world need and can identify for the Church the demands of justice. Moreover, their creative response at the local level highlights their leadership in the name of the Church and is their participation in the mission of the Lord.

Social Involvement: A Uniquely Lay Opportunity for Service

The ministry of social involvement "is so much the duty and responsibility of the laity that it can never be properly performed by others" (L 13:1). It is an area of ecclesial ministry in its own right; it is not merely demanded by the decrease in numbers of priests and religious and the despair and discouragement of some of those who remain. Rather, the apostolate of social outreach is the laity's "unique opportunity and crucial responsibility," and without it the "Church is not truly established and does not fully live."[12]

In identifying a series of components of social involvement that are typically lay services, a first dimension is the commitment to humanize our own lives and all of society's. A sense of mutual appreciation, responsible cooperation, and a willingness to work together develop human qualities in all of us. All men and women are both "haves" and "have-nots"; all are in some ways developed, underdeveloped, and depressed. Therefore, above all, lay social action brings more-human values to the fore by responding to need and challenging abuse. It calls for a new style of living that stresses above all promoting what is worthy of human dignity.

This first dimension of social action naturally leads to the ministry of cultural development as an expression of personal growth and goes hand in hand with the many social ministries of education. Cultural appreciation is for all and needs to include local and national traditions. Perhaps in our present-day global village, social ministry will need to react against mass produced culture that thwarts creativity and at times excludes moral values. One of the greatest challenges of this ministry is to integrate the values of faith and culture.[13]

Lay ministries of social outreach also include all efforts to defend the dignity of the human person by fighting for human rights, liberating the oppressed, and working for justice—for example, by ministering in developing countries and engaging in feminist causes. Involvement in defending human dignity is one of the difficult and delicate dimensions of social ministry, particularly when judicial systems protect injustice and guard the oppressors from the challenges of the oppressed. Laity also face the problem of an international Church that at times suffers from using the same oppressive methods as unjust nations and that must equally be challenged by movements of liberation. Thus we have seen laity speak out against Vatican oppression of American women religious, against the imposition of celibacy on a clergy that does not want it, against the excessive squandering of money by the international Church.

Another way laity further this ministry on behalf of human rights is through the social pressure of public opinion on civic or ecclesiastical organizations. Laity's work in the press, on television and other media, through demonstrations, gatherings, and civic or ecclesiastical disobedience can focus public attention on current violations of human rights and on policies that will lead to such violations.

Lay involvement for the just regulation of economic development is another major dimension of social outreach. Through such action laity can seek decisions that are made for the total development of the person and not merely for profit. They can seek to promote sensitivity to developing areas of the world and can promote financial aid for regions in need; and they can push for more equitable distribution of financial resources on an international level through different approaches to contracts, import tariffs, and international labor laws. Often it is inconvenient to act and easier to conform to government pressures that support the wealthy and do so on the backs of the poor. Laity will more and more be expected to speak on behalf of broad human values to world governments and businesses that are progressively more concerned with amassing wealth for a few.

Laity must commit themselves, moreover, to political issues either by running for office or by serious involvement in the few effective channels of political process (CT 75). Issues of human rights, civil liberties, legislation against discrimination, commitment to peace, moral use of taxpayers' money, and major economic policy need the pressure of political involvement to imbue them with a Christian spirit.

Effective social involvement in a lay-centered Church needs to be corporate. While individual contributions are desirable and indispensable, the major impact comes from group involvement, which often means cooperation with public or private institutions dedicated to working for justice. At times the parish can be the focus of this action,[14] but more often it is local spontaneous groups or basic ecclesial communities that have consistently seen social responsibility as part of their baptismal commitment.

The ministry of social involvement is truly prophetical insofar as it awakens people to their vocation, challenges infidelity, and gives hope for the future. It combines denunciation, compassion, and community growth. It is a way of holiness and a form of evangelization. It is at the heart of lay baptismal responsibility and effectively demonstrates the importance of a lay-centered Church.

Christianity's World Vision of Justice

A Vision from Faith

The books of world religions frequently consist of collections of teachings to be observed. Christianity, however, is a revelation of a relationship between God and the people and of new relationships between men and women precisely because of their new relationship with God. The Lord is just and acts with faithfulness, mercy, and steadfast love. Jesus, who himself embodies those qualities, reveals that the Father is rich in mercy, and his disciples are called to justice based on mercy and love.[15] Christianity is a revelation of justice, and its call for justice in every generation is "a constitutive dimension of the preaching of the Gospel."[16]

Christianity not only reveals God to humanity but also reveals the nature of humanity to men and women. It appreciates human hope, longings for justice, liberation, and peace. At the same time, it is aware of sin, selfishness, and humanity's incessant belief in fulfillment by the accumulation of possessions. Christianity knows of human need for grace and genuine liberation from greed, restlessness, and false notions of abundance.

A vision derived from faith bases life on spiritual principles that lead to integrated living, both individually and socially. Part of this vision is the realization that the world is God's gift to all humanity and that while earthly realities have autonomy, their use is intimately connected with faith.[17] In fact, men and women have a mandate from God to develop the world to the glory of God and the well-being of others. This spirituality of social involvement always places people first (CT 35:2) and knows that personal rights are generally conditioned on the needs of others (CT 69:1).

The Christian vision of justice conditions not only the essentials of spiritual life (Isaiah 58:6) but also the essentials of genuine proclamation. Evangelization necessarily includes constructive efforts for community growth and prophetical denunciation of injustice.

Faith itself challenges Christians to fulfill their civic responsibilities, furnishes insights and incentives for dedication, brings the light of revealed truth to help interpret the human condition, and calls all to integrate social commitment into the dynamics of their Christian life.

A Vision in Hope

One of the ways in which the revelation of God continues to affect the Church of every generation is the signs of the times. One way of identifying those authentic signs is to discern the consistently expressed yearnings of men and women and to confront these with the Gospel call. Their very aspirations for justice, peace, liberation, personal fulfillment, and social integration become contemporary challenges that stimulate evangelical values (CT 3:1; 44:4). Seen as signs of God's will, these are hope-filled challenges that call all Christians to make real the vision they suggest.

Another hope-filled manifestation of Christian outreach in service is the contemporary searching and stretching out for peace,[18] whether expressed individually or through organized movements. Peacemakers are committed to eradicating the causes of social unrest and injustice. Theirs is a laborious ministry of vanquishing violence and injustice at every level of social life. It is also a faith-filled conviction that such effort is not hopeless but can lead to service, trust, sharing, community growth, and universal love.[19] Like all significant ministry, the work of peacemaking is achieved locally through reconciliation, removal of dissension and distrust, and the effort to build together in family life, working conditions, local civic life, and ecumenical matters.

Christianity commits itself to social involvement because it realizes that such involvement is part of God's plan to integrate the work of building the earthly and the heavenly cities. Locally, society benefits from the Church, and the Church benefits from society. This healthy interaction is hope-filled for citizens and believers alike.

Christianity can have a leavening influence on society as a whole by making a healthy and elevating impact on the dignity of the human person and imbuing everyday human activity with meaning. The Church gives hope to the world by calling for mutual service, strengthening the family, proclaiming the need for charitable services, and challenging believers to integrate faith and daily life and to discharge civil and working obligations responsibly.

While many men and women today, individually and as nations, compulsively accumulate possessions at the expense of others, Christianity's hope-filled vision calls for detachment, simplicity, poverty, and sharing. It insists that even lawful possessions should accrue to the benefit of others (CT 69) and that the broader values of economics, culture, education, and political life are from God for the benefit of all.

A Vision of Love

Christianity confesses a God of love and compassion who challenges believers to build a global community. It introduces a new spirit into humanity, a spirit of seeing everyone as neighbor and responding enthusiastically in love. This vision is very concrete and implies an ethics of love in the daily situations of life: work, economics, politics, trade unions, government, and human dignity. In a world that stresses power, Christianity stresses service to others and dedication to promote their integral development. Christianity sees love as the answer to the problems of social conflict, and it evaluates the quality of commitment by how believers concretely work in love for others in daily life. In a world that promotes manipulation, domination, economic discrimination, and the importance of self, Christianity's vision of love stresses dialogue, cooperation, unity, communal commitment, and organized service for the benefit of everyone.

This ethic of love, while effective locally, is directed toward building a global community. It reaches out to the national and international community, believing that one encounters Jesus in all those who are hungry, thirsty, or needy in any way (Mt. 25:31–46).

Christians believe that the redemptive power of God's love must touch and heal all hurting and needy humanity (L 8:3).

This outreach is not made from the "haves" to the "have-nots" but springs from an awareness of mutual need and mutual growth. To work for others is a prime way of personal enrichment, and in satisfying the needs of others, one satisfies one's own need to reach out. Those who work for the social betterment of others may never heal society of its sin, but they will certainly bring healing to their own sinful, selfish lives.

Commitment to mutual growth must be concrete and practical and must include political commitment. It is a structured struggle against the powerbrokers of society. "What we need and hunger for are critical lovers, those who love the world intensely, as Jesus did, and so criticize it and try to correct it, as Jesus did."[20] Christian social consciousness offers an alternative way of viewing life when it insists that no matter who possesses food, it belongs to hungry people; no matter who possesses clothing, it belongs to the naked; no matter who possesses abundance, it belongs to the needy; no matter who possesses power, it must be shared with the oppressed.[21]

Christianity's world vision of justice is rooted in faith, gives the world hope, and is constructed through love.

Social Involvement and the Credibility of Christianity

The Church we love is not always faithful to the message it proclaims to others. It seems strange that the Church manages to perpetuate in some aspects of its life a reversal of biblical values—stressing power instead of service, wealth instead of poverty, status instead of universality, and law instead of freedom. The challenge to social justice is so much a constitutive dimension of its proclamation that when infidelity is seen here, the very credibility of Christianity is in question. Laity, whose ministry it is to challenge the lack of commitment to justice in social and political life,[22] frequently find themselves needing to challenge the lack of commitment to justice in ecclesiastical life.

Laity feel a sense of shame when they read of Vatican financial matters, political practices similar to those of any secular nation, pressure exerted against opposition, and discrimination against women, non-celibates, and resigned priests. Moreover, we live in a time of great distrust of Church officials, many of whom seem to have formed a party within the Church—a party made up of followers totally dedicated to the party line. It is sad to note the increased practice of reporting on fellow Christians, including bishops, to higher authorities. Some Church administrators seem to make little attempt to represent the whole Church; rather, we live in the divisiveness of theological warfare. A Church held ransom to ultraconservative leadership, itself in debt to the pressures of ultraconservative wealth, will never be credible as a modern-day evangelical witness. (Further injustices are experienced at different levels of Church life, and I have addressed these problems elsewhere.[23])

Part of social responsibility in a lay-centered Church is to help focus the Church's dedication to social justice both in the world and in the Church. In general, laity should reject all efforts to force conformity to a one-party system. Refusing to be helpless or passive, laity can outspokenly insist on their rights as baptized and can forcefully reject tendencies to an ecclesiastical totalitarianism or a dominance based on the power of the wealthy.

A major service of laity to the Church that can help intensify its credibility is to develop "an adequate theology of radical social change, particularly as this is applied to the church's own past socio-cultural work."[24] Such a theology focuses on major areas of policy and on future social commitment. Laity can then tithe to discerned areas of social need, using their financial contributions to direct social outreach. When faced with such dire world need, there is not the same urgency to contribute to internal Church funding, especially where laity may still have no voice in its use.

If the Church is to be credible to non-Christians, laity will need to work for lay rights, women's rights, priests' rights, and so on. There is a sense of oppression in the Church that has been fostered not only by the actions of the party in control but also by management practices against priests in political roles, against laity in their efforts to unionize, against liberal professors in universities, against pastors who may take liberal positions. When ecclesiastical career advancement depends more on a person's unquestioning loyalty to a specific party line than to Christianity, laity can see the need for their responsible challenge of Church management to return to the values of the Gospel rather than to follow one-sided ideologies. Challenging injustices in the Church is a painful task, but it has to be done if Christianity is to remain a credible voice for Gospel values. If we cannot find means to resolve our internal disputes; if we cannot stop attempts of subgroups to dominate; if we cannot live a respectful acknowledgement of the rights of others; if we cannot root out injustice in our own Church, how can we claim to do it for the world?

In this chapter we have reviewed Christianity's growing consciousness of its duty to be committed to social justice. We saw the call of popes in this century, have reflected on the essential nature of Christian social responsibility, and have highlighted the need for a ministry of social service. We stressed that this ministry is essentially a lay outreach, an excellent dimension of a lay-centered Church. Christianity's vision of justice comes from faith, is proclaimed in hope, and is lived as a manifestation of true Christlike love. Commitment to outreach in social justice implies serious areas of responsibility for all the baptized in a lay-centered Church. If Christians respond to this call and challenge the injustices of civil society and of the Church, Christianity will be a truly credible witness to our world.

Chapter 6

CELEBRATION AND LITURGICAL LIFE

Introduction

In the Third Gospel and the Acts, the evangelist Luke consistently emphasizes both the personal joy and enthusiasm that accompanies conversion to the Lord Jesus and the spirit of celebration that characterized the early Church communities.[1] Unfortunately, throughout the centuries Christianity in general and Catholicism in particular have not been noted for a spirit of joy and celebration. There have always been exceptional people, such as Francis of Assisi and Francis of Sales, but far too many other canonized saints portrayed a grim seriousness that became so widespread it seemed to suggest that this was Christianity's way to the Lord.

Once the period of the persecutions passed, a symbolic death for the Lord's sake was attained through ascetical practices that in turn became negative reactions to the joys of life. Marriage and sexual love, social interaction and table feasting, sports and personal fulfillment were all offered as holocausts on the altars of self-denial.

Jesus' message of joy and celebration developed into a religion that has produced enormous guilt, misery, and personal oppression. Christianity's emphasis on sin, penitence, death, purgatory, and hell, together with its development of oppressive rituals surrounding these events, has frequently perverted the simple calls of the Lord. Moreover, an outsider looking at our history would surely see that the obsession with punishment, sin, inhuman penances, negative approaches to freedom, to sex, to women, is subconsciously a form of judgment, power, and control. Even sacraments given us to celebrate the important moments of life became tainted with misery and, until recent revision, were surrounded with joyless rituals such as those of penance, anointing, and death. At times they became occasions not of joy but merely of responsibility and obligations, as in the case of the sacraments of vocation; or their reception was simply delayed, even until the point of death.

Since the time of the second Vatican Council and those years of renewal that immediately preceded it, we have witnessed a refocusing on joy, festivity, celebration, and play. We have seen spiritual renewal programs that have successfully stressed the importance of personal prayer and joyful union with the Lord. We have experienced, as never before, a rebirth of the community life of the Church. Above all, we are a generation blessed with the results of the liturgical movement. However, the integration of these developments into a celebrating Church will not take place without the vision and commitment of today's laity.

Celebrating Life

Attitudes of Celebration Rooted in Lay Life

The mission of the Church is carried out by all the baptized in their ordinary daily lives of family, work, social development, and local Church activities. However, life's ordinariness and God's awesomeness come together in celebrational worship. The prime work of all God's people is to celebrate individually and communally the worship of God.[2] But the attitudes necessary for liturgical celebration grow out of the ordinary interactions of each day. People who have difficulty celebrating life or prayer or community will have difficulty celebrating our Christian liturgy. For the latter to be truly the worship of a celebrating assembly, it must be rooted in the positive celebrational attitudes of laity in their daily lives.

Genuine worship requires cessation from work and a commitment to rest and relaxation. It is prepared for in confidence and reflection on life's experiences, in remembering former love and generosity, in stilling and silencing a yearning heart, and in concentrating on the goodness of life. It calls for a spirit of gratitude in both the individual and the family. Worship is expressed in enthusiastic praise, song, and dance. It is an opportunity to shout for joy, celebrate love, delight in the Lord. It requires paying attention, reflecting on love, applauding the wonders of God, singing and playing in the Lord, and resting in his love. Liturgy is a time of joyous festivity, of acknowledgment of gifts, of community expression of praise; it is a time of gladness spent with persons we deeply love.

Liturgical spirituality is grounded in the human values of quality of life. Liturgical celebration cannot be overlaid on a dull, uneventful, joyless, loveless, unenthusiastic life. It is in daily lay life that liturgical attitudes are formed. The worshipping assembly expresses what is already a part of life. New attitudes are rarely, if ever, generated at a Sunday service. Rather, the service is a communal expression of the attitudes of celebration lived throughout each day. The outward form of liturgy comes down to us from Church officials, but the heart and spirit of the liturgy come up from lay life.

Examples of Celebrations in Lay Life

The fostering of attitudes of celebration takes place in the basic experiences of lay life. If a spirit of celebration is not fostered at this level, it is most unlikely that it will be found at secondary or tertiary levels of Church life, such as the parish or diocese. Lay life is foundational for the community's liturgical celebrations, offering as it does so many natural and spontaneous situations where a true spirit of celebration begins. There are spontaneous and annual family celebrations, local and national celebrations and, in a country like the United States, the enriching experiences of intercultural celebrations. These are all remote preparations for liturgical life, although they are also ends in themselves.

Family celebrations of birthdays, weddings, anniversaries, first communions, confirmations, graduations, and so on, are expressed with cards, meals, dance, music, and fellowship. At times they are complemented with prayer and the sharing of stories by the older relatives. Furthermore, there are the many celebrations of a child's schooling, a spouse's career, a family's economic well-being, and a couple's love-making. There are also family celebrations of grief in disappointment, sickness, separations, divorce, and death.

In many families, each day has its own small celebrational experiences: a good-morning kiss, departures or returns from school or work, an evening meal, the narrating of a child's school day, a quiet evening, a romantic night.

On a national level, we celebrate the special events of our family and civic life, such as Mother's or Father's Day, Labor Day, the Fourth of July, Thanksgiving, and the various cultural and national feasts of our heritages.

It is at these individual, family, local, and national levels that we learn to be aware of the significance of celebration, prepare for its coming, invest and give something of ourselves for its success, participate enthusiastically, and prolong its effects for our family's or friends' benefit.

Obviously, many of these celebrations can be prepackaged by the local flower shop or greeting-card store. But these celebrations are the basis for true communal sharing. If these personal, family, local, and national expressions of celebration are prepackaged, then it is likely that the liturgy will also be prepackaged and programmed. If a true spirit of celebration pervades family and civic life, though, the people so involved will come to liturgy with the attitudes necessary for community worship. The quality of celebration in the home, or in other foundational cells of social life, will determine the quality of liturgical celebration. No miracles are worked in a Sunday service. The pastoral leader must work with what he or she finds in the pews.

Lay Celebration: Foundational for Liturgy

Since we have all attended monotonous, prepackaged, and irrelevant liturgies, we know by contrast how valuable and necessary genuine celebration is for our community worship. This century's liturgical movement produced wonderful insights and challenges culminating in the call of the Vatican Council and in those post-Conciliar renewal efforts that have resisted control by some pre-Conciliar-minded ecclesiastics. There are more signs of renewal and growth in liturgical life in the Church today than we have witnessed for centuries. However, celebration happens at the level of the local Church, where we find the power and gifts of the people. Liturgical workshops do not create celebration, nor can a skilled pastoral leader produce it when it does not already exist among the people. The primary celebrant of liturgy is the assembly of the people.[3] If the assembly has a spirit of celebration, previously generated in the members' daily lives, then the pastoral leader can channel those celebrational talents into a joyous liturgical feast.

It is interesting to see that sometimes a day of worship prescribed by Church officials is unsuccessful as a celebration. People forget to go, or at best they "fit it in"; they are not too sure of its significance in their daily lives, and they attend out of faithfulness to an obligation rather than out of enthusiasm. For most people, the Ascension and Assumption would be examples of this kind of feast. On the other hand, a celebration such as Thanksgiving day, which has no obligation prescribed for it, is often spontaneous, relevant, and prayerful, and culminates in an enthusiastic, well-attended community liturgy. Private confession is another example of a failed celebration for today, while the large congregations that attend reconciliation services attest to their success.

The way the Church celebrates is best determined from "below," by building on the attitudes of laity in the celebrations of their individual, family, and wider social life. Basic cells of lay life are not only foundational for ecclesiology but also for liturgy. Meaningful rituals of celebration are found in the home, and it is on these that the Church must build.

Celebrating Prayer

Preparations for Prayer in Lay Life

The layperson's responsible exercise of the priesthood of all the baptized culminates in an active celebration of the community's liturgy. However, as we have pointed out, that celebration is rooted in the daily attitudes of joy, hospitality, genuine presence, and love cultivated in the basic cells of lay life. Furthermore, liturgy is a *prayerful* celebration, and here too the call, growth, and quality of prayer do not develop primarily in the context of Sunday worship but in the daily contexts of lay life.

Christian spirituality has witnessed many methods of prayer growth, but many of them required time and lifestyles that were unavailable to all the baptized and were reserved to the contemplative monk or nun. This implicit put-down of lay life is based on false theology and weak spirituality.

The principal prayer of the Christian that gives glory to God is his or her total life. It is this that leads to a greater union with the Lord. Any separation between life and prayer, or between the celebration of life and the celebration of prayer, is an unhealthy one, as is any understanding of prayer that requires an elitist lifestyle and exceptional preparations. Any time set aside for intensified prayer is based on fundamental attitudes that cannot be switched on or off but are life attitudes lived throughout each moment of the day and intensified in so-called prayer periods.

Genuine prayer requires the Christian to live true charity, give prime time to the more intense periods of prayer, and choose a place for prayer that is conducive to an experience of the Lord. The Christian's contribution is secondary and is best seen in the way he or she cultivates throughout daily life those basic attitudes that enable a person to be still and available to the Lord, facilitate an openness to the Spirit's inspiration, lead to concentration in Christ, and prepare for the rich religious experience of silence in God. The quality and growth of prayer are principally the work of the Lord, who takes the initiative in calling us to pray. Our growth in prayer is not earned by commitment to exceptional methods nor restricted to clerical or religious vocational commitments.

The kernel of contemplative prayer is silence in God. There are several attitudes of daily life that can undoubtedly help in acquiring it. Prayer requires stillness. We need to sit still, do nothing, and completely relax. Any technique for relaxation that helps us acquire stillness in the presence of God can be used. In our present restless age, stillness can be a real asceticism, and yet it is a healthy part of everyone's life. It is not something that can be turned on for moments of prayer; it is acquired very gradually through self-training in the context of daily life.

In addition to stillness, prayer requires openness to the inspirations of the Holy Spirit. If we are to be open to those inspirations in times of prayer, it will be because we have developed in daily life an attitude of total attentiveness to ourselves, to our family and friends, to our world's needs. This openness extends to the Spirit who speaks to us in our own hearts and through Scripture, the Church, others, and the daily events of our history. Without a habitually listening heart it is humanly impossible for us to switch on to the inspirations of the Holy Spirit in times of prayer.

Concentration is an art needed both in prayer and in daily life. If we train ourselves to concentrate in daily life, we will be able to concentrate in Christ in prayer. For laity, concentration is part of family life, work, friendship, and success in professional development. Awareness of the presence of others, recollection, a sense of wonder and astonishment, an openness to the unexpected, patience in loneliness, and a willingness to wait are beautiful qualities of daily life that are excellent preparations for prayer.[4] All forms of concentration, whether on a beautiful scene, on the conversation of others, on the needs of a child, on the expressions of love for a spouse, or on the requirements of a job, develop faculties that can be used in a prayerful concentration on God.

In short, to prepare ourselves for the prayerful celebration of the community's liturgy, there is no better method than a commitment to the essential requirements of lay life.

Lay Life's Opportunities for Growth in Prayer

We are all responsible for our growth in prayer, but Christian history documents little emphasis on prayer for laity. Moreover, most prayer methods were developed by celibates for celibates and seemed to exclude the possibility that the advanced stages in prayer growth were available to laity. Nowadays, however, we stress the universal call to holiness and fullness of life; we see the close connection between human self-realization and prayer, and growth in prayer as not only available to but actually necessary for us all.

Prayer is the work of God in us, and we cannot force it or squeeze out of ourselves sentiments that are really not ours. Nevertheless, prayer is essentially the Spirit's expressions through us, and the same Spirit is in us all, so that "Between the great, unfailing prayer of the Church and the hesitant, groping prayer of the individual, there is an unbreakable bond."[5]

For every baptized person, prayer is the vital expression of his or her total personality. If one's life is empty, uncommitted, and unfulfilled, prayer will assuredly be weak. Laity who live lives full of joy, peace, humor, creativity, and spontaneity, who are open to new experiences, who have many interests, extensive friendships, and commitment to world development also have the possibility of very healthy prayer lives. Prayer and integrated human development wax or wane together.

During periods of intensified prayer, we see more clearly our true selves and learn to accept ourselves.[6] Insofar as prayer helps us see ourselves as we are and accept ourselves, it leads to authentic, integrated living. In contemplative prayer, where we see and accept ourselves as children of God, we anticipate our future union with God. Also, in prayer we grow as persons, for we see and accept our abilities and talents, knowing that we can contribute much good to others in social development, to the Church, and to the world around us through apostolic commitment.[7] All these dimensions of prayer are readily available to all the baptized.

Part of the self-acceptance that comes in prayer is the acceptance of one's sinfulness, which, when linked to the desire to change, is another component of prayer-growth. In prayer our natural creaturely attitude of total dependence, insignificance, and helplessness is intensified by the awareness of our rebellion and opposition to the Lord in sin. Hence, among the initial attitudes required for prayer we find this acceptance of one's sinfulness, along with the desire to change seen in reconciliation, repentance, and an initial conversion.

Prayer is a total self-direction to the Lord that is a point of departure for healthy self-realization. We can really be who we are in the presence of God who is. We really are free to be and become our true selves. God accepts me as I am, with all the areas within me that have not yet been transformed. In mature prayer, every aspect of life becomes of prayer value, and the whole of existence becomes prayerful insofar as it is permeated by life-attitudes of adoration, thanksgiving, sorrow, petition, and love.

All forms of prayer—formal worship, group, family and individual contemplative prayer—imply a challenge for the future, insofar as we are always called to work to attain what we pray for. This work to attain our desired future develops qualities in us that would otherwise remain only latent. In prayer of intercession we ask the Lord to answer a certain request. However, if our prayer is not going to be mere escapism or a using of God to fill gaps in life that we cannot handle, then the prayer of request will be complemented with our effort to bring about the attaining of the request. This effort develops untapped aspects of our personality.[8]

In prayer we open ourselves to the action of the Spirit within us and actualize the greatest aspects of our personalities. It is principally in prayer that we live as true children of God, become aware that we are part of God's family, and are challenged to live as community. When we look at the preparations for prayer and the relationships between prayer and self-realization, we see that lay life offers excellent opportunities to celebrate the life of prayer.

Celebrating Community

Conversion to Community

A contemporary trend in spirituality is the growing awareness that Christian conversion implies a commitment to community growth. Many of the spiritual movements of recent years, such as Focolare, Cursillo, and Movement for a Better World, emphasize sharing in faith, witness of mutual charity, and the communal dimension of spirituality.[9] Although spiritual life used to be viewed as something very individualistic, it is now concerned also with the community's searching together for God.[10]

However, just as there are stages in an individual's conversion and maturing as a Christian, so also there are stages in a group's development. Certain Christian practices are important in our individual journey to the Lord, but there are also practices and attitudes particularly appropriate for our community conversion to the Lord. Moreover, laity are specially gifted to experience these in their ordinary daily interactions with others and can thereby capitalize on daily life experiences for their conversion to Christian community.

The first stage in a communal conversion is awareness of being community.[11] This awareness of being part of a group is a formative power in itself and leads to the conviction that only by sharing with others in community and risking life with them can we realize our full potential. This religious appreciation of community can be readily based on the lay experience of family life, networking, sharing in professional groups, and civic responsibility.

Once people come together in community, there follows a stage when they develop interpersonal relationships. This requires that each participant develop his or her basic human qualities. This second stage in communal conversion is foundational for all further growth, whether on a parish or wider ecclesial level. The more deeply we relate to people with courtesy, kindness, pleasantness, gentleness, and patience, the more easily we eventually enter into deeper sharing in faith.

Third, no matter how much we are aware of the community dimension of life or give ourselves to developing basic human qualities, a group's growth is often hindered by our poor unconscious attitudes. These must be surfaced and removed before we can grow. Many helpful techniques are learned by laity in pre-marriage preparation, in work or family counseling, and from their experience as spouses, parents, and work supervisors. This third stage is best dealt with after human relationships are well established.

A fourth stage in communal conversion is a clear interest in the community's life. This means being interested in the total group and in each individual in the group, and it may well require simple structures of group sharing, such as group reports, to manifest interest and concern for each member.[12] It will also require time commitment, attentiveness, and quality presence to each one. Like the previous stages, this one requires qualities that laity already need to develop in their friendships and in their family, professional, and wider civic life.

Fifth, a major stage in conversion to community is the acceptance of responsibility for others in the group. This means listening, supporting, challenging, and correcting others in a spirit of love and respect, accompanied by a willingness to take risks and possibly be rejected.

The sixth stage in living and celebrating community is a studied practice of community. This will mean sharing life in meetings and time together; sharing vision and ideals in group reflection and study; sharing faith in its many experiences; sharing prayer, meditation, liturgy, and apostolic involvement in planning.[13]

Reviewing the stages of conversion to community—an awareness of being community, a development of basic human qualities, the uncovering of unconscious attitudes, the fostering of interest in the group, a responsibility for all the members, and a studied practice of community—we find that laity in their daily lives already have these experiences and this expertise to enrich communal celebrations of prayer and community life.

Lay Responsibilities to Build Community

The first responsibility the baptized have regarding the integration of a community dimension into their Christian lives is to themselves, since growth in community is also part of our own personal well-being. We develop through interaction with others, not only because such interaction helps us overcome possible loneliness, alienation from society, personal isolation, and a sense of rootlessness, but also because it draws out of each of us our potentials for sensitivity to others' needs, for being available, for balance between belonging and personal autonomy, and for cooperation with others in a common endeavor. This interaction in community gives us a chance to share our concerns, to develop close friendships, to find respect and appreciation, to enjoy satisfaction in mutual interdependence. In doing so, our own personalities are enriched and made more human.

Second, community building is a true asceticism that demands the death of individualism and leads to a liberation from our false defenses and the development of a new spiritual presence with others in friendship.[14] Unlike depersonalizing competition, sharing enriches our humanity. After all, "Amongness, not upness, is the dynamic of the spiritual journey."[15]

Third, as a community, believers are also responsible for the Word on which their life is built and by which they are nourished. The fact that they are bound together in a common spirit helps prepare them to receive the Word and leads them to a common commitment to carry out its challenge. It is in light of the Word that communities clarify their shared vision and discern the needs that call for their common response.[16] This is often best achieved through the simple structures of primary groups such as families or basic ecclesial communities, where laity who are at the cutting edge of the Church's mission can clearly identify real needs, and also at the secondary level of parishes, through their councils, by raising "their own consciousness and the consciousness of the total parish community of the responsibility of all baptized members to be ministers."[17]

This responsibility to clarify a shared vision and discern needs leads to a community outreach in ministry.[18] This fourth responsibility in community growth is very significant, since nowadays the more significant forms of ministry are carried out by lay groups that respond to the individual, family, and other social needs of their neighbors.[19] They are ministers to human need and prophets of denunciation against social injustice.

Fifth, community living also implies responsibility for leadership. In their various family or professional groups, laity are accustomed to the need to identify and provide leaders who can achieve the goals of the group. While we don't want an "ecclesiastical tyranny . . . where the majority vote of the faithful decides everything,"[20] neither do we want the continuation of ever-increasing numbers of priestless communities. The lay experience is again a corrective that leads to finding other leaders for many priestless communities. In fact, even many communities with a priest have found their leaders elsewhere.

Our liturgies are prayerful celebrations of the community. Each component of the communal worship—such as friendship, joy, peace, creativity, family love, and prayer—is rooted in lay life, as we have seen. The pastoral leader needs to identify the dimensions of worship in the daily experiences of all the baptized. He or she must appreciate the faithful's ability to celebrate life and celebrate prayer and must draw them together in the assembly. But the very experience of community is basically a lay aspect of the Church. Awareness, understanding, commitment, and responsibility for community growth are daily needs of laity. These skills are brought together in the prayerful celebration of worship, so that out of the diverse groups a supra-community can be built up. However, pastoral practice must focus more on the Church's *source* of celebration, prayer, and community, and must develop new skills to surface the life that comes from the laity rather than filtering it down from the hierarchy.

Celebrating Worship

Components of Liturgical Spirituality

The second Vatican Council moved away from any elitist approach to spirituality and instead presented the universal call to holiness. The sacramental system of the Church was seen as the basis for all spiritual growth. Growth in holiness is celebrated and deepened in the liturgical life in which we all share, and is made concrete for each person by the sacraments of vocation.[21] All laity are called to take an active part in the Church's liturgical life, especially the Eucharist, to focus their renewal on the liturgical year, and to express their faith through ecclesial prayer.[22]

The covenant is made with the whole people and not just with their priestly ministers. Thus the liturgy becomes the central expression of the whole covenanted people's commitment to the Lord.[23] For this reason, community worship is the celebration of the entire assembly that accepts its shared responsibility for the liturgy; it is not just a passive audience but an actively involved assembly that appreciates the values proclaimed and celebrated.[24]

The involvement of all the people leads to "the transformation of the assembly," which is "ultimately more fundamental than the transformation of the bread and wine, for it is crucial to the message and mission of Christ."[25]

This transformation of the assembly has four stages: the conscious gathering with others in Christian hospitality to celebrate together the previous week's own nonliturgical celebrations; the prayerful listening to each other, to each one's needs, to the world, and especially to the Word in the Church; the generous and faith-filled sharing in building the ecclesial community through the Eucharist; the prophetic outreach by means of the community's communal ministry.[26]

The liturgical celebration of the Word and of God's saving actions in history is both the culmination of life and the beginning of a new phase of life for all the baptized. It capitalizes on the qualities that believers bring to it, but through interaction with others in faith it also creates dispositions where they are not already present and brings them to fruition in mutual growth and practical commitment in the marketplaces of life.

Every baptized Christian comes to worship bringing his or her life of celebration, prayer, and community building and lives out the ritual gestures of sharing, caring, attentive presence, and mutual commitment. The believer then goes forth to witness to celebration, to arouse prayer in others, to build small communities and large societies, and to be a visionary interpreter and a prophetic challenger of our world. The liturgy thus becomes the basic form of spiritual renewal for all laity and their way of sharing in the priestly, prophetic, and servant functions of Jesus.

For liturgical spirituality to be sound and fruitful, the assembly must be able to respond to the following questions: "Is the eucharistic prayer experienced as praying? Who prays the prayer? What is the thrust of the praying? In what context do we praise God? What happens to us as a consequence?"[27] If the liturgy is our prime prayer, and if we knowingly, actively, and fruitfully participate in corporate gratitude for the blessings of the Lord and in generous self-gift to others, then we become more and more the body of Christ, and the liturgy becomes the great spiritual enrichment of our lives.

Assessment of Today's Liturgies

Most Catholic people encounter the Church in liturgical gatherings. The image portrayed there is Catholicism for them; where the celebration is merely orchestrated by the pastoral leader, it often portrays a passive Church or a minor version of the contemporary electronic Church instead of the celebration of all the baptized. This kind of approach, where the liturgy is simply someone's show, is partly the result of the orientation of the Latin Roman canon, with its distance, silence, unintelligibility, and passive audience.

Even today, after years of development since Vatican II, we often have a chameleon model of pastoral leader who moves from quiet, passively attended early morning Sunday services to a spectacularly orchestrated noon Mass.

In spite of considerable effort on both sides, we still have much passivity, inertia, and apathy, frequently because of the permanence of a them/us distinction between officiating clergy and attending congregation.[28] Moreover, the most common reaction to liturgical renewal has been indifference and a minimalistic, passive implementation of suggested change.[29] Furthermore, one of the U.S. bishops' committees concluded, "We must point out that the parish activity least often directly addressed in parish development programs we have reviewed is the liturgy."[30]

Liturgy, the sacraments in particular, is not as central in spiritual life as it should be. In the early Church, sacraments satisfied the people's felt needs, whereas now laity have to be told they need the sacraments. Lack of lay appreciation is partly due to their inadequate knowledge of religious education, but it is also a result of a growing irrelevance of present rituals. As a result, some laity merely attend mechanically what for them are sterile liturgies.

Pastoral leadership, especially in liturgy, is an increasingly difficult task that requires flexibility, insight, good theological training, and practical leadership skills. In New Testament times, the person who led the community celebrated the liturgy, but now the person who celebrates the Eucharist is expected to lead the community. In past decades, the priestly ministers were the best qualified of the people and excellently prepared to lead the assembly. Seminary graduates today, however, in general, are less educated, less balanced, less experienced, and more insecure than large numbers of their congregations.

In many parishes today, the assembly must deal with the complete absence of a priestly minister to celebrate the community's worship. Without this support from their Church and its official leaders, these communities are often left to find their own way of worship or to cope somehow with the absence of what they have been trained to acknowledge as essential.

Left to their own resources as many laity are today, either because of the absence of a priest or because of the imposition of an unqualified priest, laity are becoming more aware than ever that they have practically no formation at all in individual or liturgical prayer suited to today's world. Diluted versions of the spirituality or prayer of religious are clearly inadequate for the challenging world of today's laity.

Vital and essential though liturgical spirituality is, there are increasing obstacles to the community's worship: lack of active participation, consumeristic searching for what appeals, a substantial gap between clergy and laity, the growing irrelevance of today's rituals, poor leadership or no leadership at all, and a serious lack of lay approaches to prayer, worship, and spirituality in general.

Celebrating Worship in a Lay-Centered Church

The main thesis of this book, as we have seen in the final sections of each chapter, is that laity themselves must take responsibility for their Church. Likewise, in celebrating worship, laity must always presume that they have something significant to offer when they reflect on their life experiences. They need to be aware of their personal baptismal call to be committed to prayer growth and to the responsible development of local community life. Above all, laity will need to anticipate and develop their own rhythms in liturgy, as they do in everyday life.

Sadly, laity need to expect less from Sunday services than they have been accustomed to. Some even need an ability to worship in spite of the liturgy.[31] However, they must not have liturgy dictated to them, nor be pressured by legalism, but rather decide what is a meaningful liturgy for themselves, their family, and friends.

Since there are now few experts "out there" but generally only other Christians in the same assembly sharing responsibility for worship, laity will need to think in different terms regarding what constitutes quality in community life and in their celebration of life and of prayer. This will turn their attention to the celebrational experiences of their families and basic ecclesial communities and let their values percolate upwards to the parish.

In attending parish services, laity need not be afraid to filter out of the celebration only what is suitable and beneficial for themselves. They should responsibly evaluate the liturgical performance of all participants and go to other parishes for their community worship if necessary. Clearly they should not accept a leadership that is not worthy of their support.

In some places, laity will need to presume that there will rarely be a priest present so they should courageously surface their own liturgical leaders and create their own forms of community prayer.[32] The community will also need to increase its awareness of its obligation to provide community leaders suitable to today's circumstances. In the short run, this should mean more lay involvement in seminary training, rather than the current situation of field training provided by laity after the new priest has arrived in the parish.[33]

The parish is a community of communities, and this is precisely the case in worship too. The quality of parish worship in a lay-centered Church depends on the quality of prayerful celebration in one's own individual life and on the quality of community life in family and neighborhood cell groups. The prime lay responsibility is local, and if the foundation is well laid, there will be reasons to hope for growth in celebrational worship at all other levels of ecclesial life.

NOTES

CHAPTER 1. RECENT DEVELOPMENTS REGARDING LAITY

1. See Leonard Doohan, *The Lay-Centered Church* (Minneapolis: Winston Press, 1984), pp. 1–4.
2. See *Lay-Centered Church*, pp. 43–53.
3. See Avery Dulles, *Models of the Church* (New York: Doubleday and Co., Inc., 1974); *The Resilient Church* (New York: Doubleday and Co., Inc., 1977); *A Church to Believe In* (New York: Crossroad, 1982); Bernard Besret, *Tomorrow a New Church* (New York: Paulist Press, 1973); Johann Baptist Metz, *The Emergent Church* (New York: Crossroad, 1981).
4. See Dulles, *Models of the Church;* "Imaging the Church for the 1980s," *Thought*, 56 (1981): 121–138; Roger D. Haight, "Mission: The Symbol for Understanding the Church Today," *Theological Studies* 37 (1976): 620–649.
5. See *Lay-Centered Church*, pp. 4–23.
6. See Avery Dulles, *Models of the Church*, pp. 151–165; James A. Coriden, "The Contours of Ministry," *Social Thought* Fall (1980): 3–9; "Options for the Organization of Ministry," *Jurist* 41 (1981): 480–501; Robert L. Kinast, *Caring for Society: A Theological Interpretation of Lay Ministry* (Chicago: The Thomas More Press, 1985).
7. See *Lay-Centered Church*, ch. 3 pp. 62–89.
8. See *Lay-Centered Church*, pp. 111–119.
9. "The Chicago Declaration of Christian Concern," in *Challenge to the Laity*, Russell Barta, ed., Huntington, Indiana: Our Sunday Visitor, 1980, p. 21.
10. "Chicago Declaration," p. 23.
11. See "Chicago Declaration," p. 22–23.
12. See "Chicago Declaration," p. 20.
13. See "Chicago Declaration, p. 24.
14. See "Chicago Declaration, pp. 9–17, and all articles in Barta (ed.), *Challenge to the Laity* (note 9).
15. Arthur Jones, "Bishops: Laity Invisible to the World," *National Catholic Reporter*, 30 March 1979, p. 12.
16. See Coriden, "Options," pp. 480–501; David Noel Power, "The Basis for Official Ministry in the Church," *Jurist* 41 (1981): 314–342; Edward Schillebeeckx, "The Christian Community and Its Office-Bearers," *Concilium* 133 (1980): 95–133; *Ministry* (New York: Crossroad, 1981).
17. See Coriden, "Options," pp. 480–501.
18. See John Paul II, "Apostolic Exhortation on the Family," *Origins* 11 (1981): 437–468; "On Human Work" *(Laborem Exercens)*, *Origins* 11 (1981): 225–244; U. S. Bishops, "Called and Gifted: Catholic Laity 1980," *Origins* 10 (1980): 369–373; "The Challenge of Peace: God's Promise and Our Response," *Origins* 13 (1983): 1–32; *Code of Canon Law* (Washington, D.C.: Canon Law Society

of America, 1983); U. S. Bishops, "Catholic Social Teaching and the U. S. Economy," *Origins* 14 (1984): 337-383; Synod of Bishops, *Vocation and Mission of the Laity in the Church and in the World Twenty Years after the Second Vatican Council* (Vatican City 1985).
19. See John Naisbitt, *Megatrends* (New York: Warner Books, Inc., 1982).
20. Canons 208-223 list the rights common to all the baptized, and Canons 224-231 deal specifically with the rights of laity. To these can be added Canons 298, 299, and 321-329, which deal with laity's rights to form associations.
21. See the commentary by Kenneth E. Lasch, "Personnel Issues," *Code, Community, Ministry,* James H. Provost, ed. (Washington, D.C.: Canon Law Society of America, 1983), p. 69.
22. See Canons 514 and 536.
23. See Laurence J. O'Connell, "God's Call to Humankind: Towards a Theology of Vocation," *Chicago Studies* 18 (1979): 147-159; Synod of Bishops, *Vocation and Mission,* No. 16.
24. See Karl Rahner, *The Shape of the Church to Come* (New York: The Seabury Press, 1972), chs. 3 and 4 of part II and chs. 3 and 4 of part III.
25. Matthew Fox, "Teaching the Spirituality of Jesus: A Vision and a Blueprint," National Conference of Diocesan Directors of Religious Education, 1975 (duplicated notes), p. 2.
26. See John Shelby Spong, "The Emerging Church: A New Form for a New Era," *Christian Century* 96 (1979): 10-16.
27. See Marcel Uylenbroeck, "Lay Associations in the Church," *L'Osservatore Romano* (English edition), 18 August 1977, p. 8.
28. See Robert McClory, "Chicago Laity Meet; Results Mixed," *National Catholic Reporter,* 3 July 1981, p. 2. Rosemary Ruether, "Matters Left Unsaid," *Commonweal* 105 (1978): 113, states explicitly: "There have not been lacking some dynamic lay movements in my recent Catholic experience. . . . Not one has had anything but a negative relation with the hierarchical Church."
29. See for example, Dulles, *Reslient Church*; *A Church to Believe In*; Hans Küng, "Participation of the Laity in Church Leadership and in Church Elections," *Journal of Ecumenical Studies* 6 (1969): 511-533.
30. See, for example, Edward Schillebeeckx, "The Christian Community and Its Office-Bearers," pp. 95-133; Richard P. McBrien, "The Nature and Use of Power in the Church," *Catholic Theological Society of America Proceedings* 37 (1982): 38-49; William J. Bausch, *Traditions, Tensions, Transitions in Ministry* (Mystic, Connecticut: Twenty-Third Publications, 1982), ch. 2: "From Prophet to Presbyter to Priest"; Thomas Franklin O'Meara, *Theology of Ministry* (New York: Paulist Press, 1983), ch. 5: "The Metamorphoses of Ministry."
31. See the annotated bibliography on leadership in Helen Doohan, *Leadership in Paul* (Wilmington, Delaware: Michael Glazier Inc., 1984), pp. 173-193.
32. See Terrence Dosh, "Clericalism," *Ministries* 2 (Oct. 1981): 20-23. H. J. Pottmeyer, "Pastoral Service: Laity and Priest," *Theology Digest* 27 (1979): 53, comments: "Given a dualistic concept of pastoral ministry (active office holders and passive church members), all those who play an active role in church life will inevitably be seen as 'clergy,' not 'people.'"

33. See Howard C. Blake, "Styles in Christian Missions," *The New Laity*, Ralph D. Bucy, ed. (Waco, Texas: Word Books, 1978), p. 182.
34. See *Lay-Centered Church*, pp. 28–38.
35. See Jacques Mulders, "After the Dutch Synod," *The Month* 13 (1980): 189–194.
36. See Dulles, *A Church to Believe In*, p. 145.
37. See Dulles, *A Church to Believe In*, p. 116; also Edward John Kilmartin, "Lay Participation in the Apostolate of the Hierarchy," *Jurist* 41 (1981): 369; "Episcopal Election: The Right of the Laity," *Concilium* 137 (1980): 39–43.
38. See Schillebeeckx, "Christian Community and Its Office-Bearers," p. 121.
39. See Jean Guitton, *The Church and the Laity* (New York: Alba House, 1965), pp. 49–60; also Donald Nicodemus, *The Democratic Church* (Milwaukee: The Bruce Publishing Co., 1968), pp. 37–51.
40. For an explanation of "non-acceptatio legis" see George V. Lobo, *Guide to Christian Living: A New Compendium of Moral Theology* (Westminster, Maryland: Christian Classics, 1984), p. 253; also Philip A. Ballinger, *The Ecclesiological Reality of "Reception."* Thesis presented at Katholieke Universiteit Leuven, 1984, especially pp. 55–62, where the author gives excellent documentation.
41. Dulles, "Imaging the Church for the 1980's," p. 126.
42. Schillebeeckx, "Christian Community and Its Office-Bearers," p. 121.
43. See John A. Coleman, "Toward a Church with a Worldly Vocation," *Challenge to the Laity*, Russell Barta, ed., p. 84; also Dennis Geaney, *Full Church, Empty Rectory* (Notre Dame, Indiana: Fides/Claretian, 1980), p. 24.
44. Dulles, "Imaging the Church," p. 123; see also Juan Luis Segundo, *The Community Called Church* (New York: Orbis Books, 1973), p. vii.
45. See Karl G. Schmude, "Towards a Lay Spirituality," *Communio* 6 (1979): 365–377.
46. See Andrew Greeley, Mary Durkin and others, *Parish, Priest and People* (Chicago: The Thomas More Press, 1981), p. 204.
47. See Otto Ter Reegen, "The Rights of the Laity," *Concilium* 38 (1968): 17–30.
48. See Dolores Leckey, "What the Laity Need," *Origins* 12 (1982): 9–15.

CHAPTER 2. LAITY AND THE LOCAL CHURCH

1. John Paul II, "Redeemer of Man" *(Redemptor Hominis)*, *Origins* 8 (1979): 631.
2. See Robert C. Dixon and Dean R. Hoge, "Models and Priorities of the Catholic Church as Held by Suburban Laity," *Review of Religious Research* 20 (1979): 150–167; The feeling of non-belonging is mutual, as the Synod of Bishops *Vocation and Mission*, No. 7, raises the problem of the laity's "ecclesiality": "to what extent, and especially with regard to their temporal activity, can the laity be considered as authentic expressions of the Church."
3. For considerations on the use of the terms "particular Church" and "local Church" see Sabbas J. Kilian, "The Meaning and Nature of Local Church, *Catholic Theological Society of America Proceedings* 35 (1980): 244–255, and Patrick Granfield, "The Local Church as a Center of Communication

and Control," *Catholic Theological Society of America Proceedings* 35 (1980): 256–263.
4. See Granfield, p. 258.
5. See *John Paul II and the Laity*, Leonard Doohan, ed. (New York: Le Jacq Publishing, Inc., 1984), p. 132; also David M. Thomas, *The Prophetic Role of the Christian Family: A Proposal for the Foundational Church*, a document prepared for the Pre-Synod Consultation, University of Notre Dame, 15–18 June 1980.
6. See "The Synod on the Family Begins", 26 September 1980, in *Origins* 10 (1980): 259.
7. Thomas, p. 6.
8. See the articles on local Church in *Catholic Theological Society of America Proceedings* 35 (1980) and 36 (1981).
9. See Granfield, p. 258.
10. John Paul II, "Address to the Bishops of Papua, New Guinea and the Solomon Islands," *L'Osservatore Romano*, 5 November 1979, p. 13; quoted by Granfield, p. 259.
11. Naisbitt, *Megatrends*, p. 191.
12. See Dulles, "Imaging the Church for the 1980s," p. 123.
13. See Robert Schreiter, "Local Theologies in the Local Church: Issues and Methods," *Catholic Theological Society of America Proceedings* 36 (1981): 96–112.
14. Schillebeeckx, "Christian Community and Its Office-Bearers," p. 124.
15. See Schillebeeckx, "Christian Community and Its Office-Bearers," p. 118.
16. See William J. Rademacher, "The History of the Parish," *Answers for Parish Councillors* (Mystic, Connecticut: Twenty-Third Publications, 1981), p. 19.
17. See Rademacher, p. 24.
18. See, for example, David O. Moberg, "What the Graying of America Means to the Local Church," *Christianity Today* 25 (1981): 1579–1582.
19. See the documents of Vatican II: C 12:3; 30:2; 37; L 10; 22; also Philip J. Murnion, "The Parish Community: Theological Questions Arising from Attempts to Implement Vatican II," *Catholic Theological Society of America Proceedings* 36 (1981): 39–55; U.S. Bishops' Committee on the Parish, "The Parish: A People, a Mission, a Structure," *Origins* 10 (1981): 641–645.
20. See Ernest Larkin, ed. *Spiritual Renewal of American Priesthood* (Washington, D.C.: USCC., 1973), p. 16.
21. See Bausch, *Traditions*, p. 121; Greeley and others, *Parish, Priest and People*; Bishop Thomas Murphy of Great Falls-Billings, "On Parish Councils and Lay Ministry," *Origins* 11 (1982): 650–651.
22. See interim report of U.S. Bishops' ad hoc committee on the parish, "Dimensions of Parish Renewal," *Origins* 9 (1980): 566–569; Bausch, *Traditions*, pp. 121–122.
23. Dennis Geaney, *Full Church, Empty Rectory*, p. 22: quoting John R. Gilbert.
24. Peter Rudge, quoted by Bausch, *Traditions*, p. 122.
25. Jürgen Moltmann, "The Diaconal Church in the Context of the Kingdom of God," *Hope for the Church* (Nashville: Abingdon Press, 1979), p. 21; see also Rademacher, ch. 3: "The Future of the Parish," pp. 39–50.

26. See Doohan, *Lay-Centered Church*, p. 68, for descriptions and conciliar references.
27. *Lay-Centered Church*, p. 84.
28. See Johann Baptist Metz, "Base-Church and Bourgeois Religion," *Theology Digest* 29 (1981): 203–206; Alvaro Barriero, *Basic Ecclesial Communities: The Evangelization of the Poor* (New York: Orbis Books, 1982).
29. See *John Paul II and the Laity*, p. 67.
30. See Coleman, "Toward a Church with a Worldly Vocation," p. 93.
31. See documents of Vatican II, L 10; 17; 26; B 27; 30; M 21; 30.
32. See Dennis Geaney, "Layman Directs College's Pastoral Ministry," *National Catholic Reporter*, 19 January 1979, p. 7, quoting a Church official saying "Laity have no authority in the decision-making process of the church, and in my view it will be a sad day when they do."

CHAPTER 3. WORK

1. For the works of these theologians and others, see the detailed bibliography on laity in *Lay-Centered Church*, pp. 156–165.
2. See Richard P. McBrien, *Church: The Continuing Quest*, pp. 14–21.
3. See Ed Marciniak, "On the Condition of the Laity," *Challenge to the Laity*, pp. 30, 36.
4. See C 48:3; CT 11:1; Edward Schillebeeckx, *God the Future of Man* (New York: Sheed and Ward, 1969), p. 78: "Commitment to this world, experienced as faith, thus forms an essential part of the Christian faith in God."
5. All the baptized in their work are continuing God's creative actions. God left his work unfinished, as the symbolic number six indicates in the creation story, and God is portrayed expectantly waiting to see what man and woman would do to develop and enrich creation, as the symbolic gesture of naming the creatures indicates. Jesus too refers to his ministry and miracles as "works." See Raymond E. Brown, *New Testament Essays* (New York: Image Books, 1968), p. 234.
6. See CT 11:2; 15:2; 16:3; 25:3; 37; 40:4; 78:2, 7.
7. Alfons Auer, *Open the World* (Dublin: Gill and Son, 1966), p. 125.
8. See C 31; CT 34:1; 43; 57:2; L 7:5.
9. See Auer, p. 216: "The indolent renunciation of discovery and utilization of created potentials destroys the honour of God on earth and the completion by mankind of his divinely willed being and his God-given task."
10. See C 36:6; L 7:5.
11. See C 42:8; CT 37:5; M. D. Chenu, *The Theology of Work* (Dublin: Gill and Son, 1963), p. 8; Karl Rahner, "The Order of Redemption within the Order of Creation," *Mission and Grace* (New York: Sheed and Ward, 1963), vol. 1, p. 97.
12. See *Chicago Declaration of Christian Concern*; Arthur Jones, "Bishops: Laity Invisible to the World," p. 12, 14.
13. See John Paul II, "On Human Work" *(Laborem Exercens)*, *Origins* 11 (1981): 230.

14. See M 11:3; L 7:3; CT 57:5; Paul VI, "Address to FAO," *L'Osservatore Romano* (English edition), 26 November 1970, p. 6: "The most extraordinary scientific progress, the most astounding technical feats and the most amazing economic growth, unless accompanied by authentic moral and social progress, will in the long run go against man."
15. Joseph Komonchak, "Clergy, Laity, and the Church's Mission in the World," *Jurist* 41 (1981): 447.
16. Barbara Brown Zikmund, "Christian Vocation—In Context," *Theology Today* 36 (1979–80): 335.
17. Brown Zikmund, p. 335.
18. Brown Zikmund, p. 335.
19. See *John Paul II and the Laity*, pp. 122–125.
20. This section is a summary of the encyclical of Pope John Paul II, "On Human Work" *(Laborem Exercens)*, *Origins* 11 (1981): 225–244, especially pp. 228–232.
21. See *U.S. News and World Report* 21 February 1977, and 15 January 1979.
22. See Hugo Rahner, *Man at Play* (New York: Herder and Herder, 1967); Harvey Cox, *The Feast of Fools* (New York: Harper & Row, 1970); Leonard Doohan, "The Spiritual Value of Leisure," *Spirituality Today* 31 (1979): 157–167.
23. Edward Fitzgerald, "A Time for Play?" *Clergy Review* 59 (1974): 283.
24. See Matthew Fox, *Whee! We, Wee, All the Way Home: A Guide to the New Sensual Spirituality*, (Santa Fe: Bear and Co., 1976), ch. 1.
25. See Cox, chs. 1 and 4.
26. Fitzgerald, p. 337.
27. Roman Bleisten, "Leisure," *Sacramentum Mundi*, vol. 3 p. 300.
28. Bleisten, p. 300.
29. See John Paul II, "Work and Prayer: A Necessary Alliance in the Soul," *Origins* 9 (1979): 72: "In every human work prayer sets up a reference to God the creator and redeemer, and it also contributes to complete 'humanization' of work."
30. See John Paul II, "The Vatican and Its Employees," *Origins* 12 (1982): 418–421; also "The Workbench of Life," *Origins* 13 (1984): 593–602.
31. See *Lay-Centered Church*, pp. 111–119.
32. See CT 35.
33. See Marciniak, *Challenge*, p. 38.

CHAPTER 4. FAMILY

1. These trends are taken from a public address given by Dr. David Thomas at Gonzaga University, Spokane, Washington, 30 March 1984.
2. See Leonard Doohan, ed., *John Paul II and the Laity* (New York: Le Jacq Publishing, 1984), pp. 129–130.
3. This support was given most recently by John Paul II, "The Apostoloic Exhortation on the Family," *Origin* 11 (1981): 443.
4. For a fine reflection on the spirituality of the domestic Church, see Mitch and Kathy Finley, *Christian Families in the Real World* (Chicago: The Thomas

More Press, 1984); also Annetta T. Wallace, "Ongoing Marriage: Maintaining the Awe," *Studies in Formative Spirituality* 6 (1985): 271-282.
5. See Evelyn Eaton Whitehead and James D. Whitehead, "Sexuality and Intimacy in Marriage," *Chicago Studies* 18 (1979): 255.
6. See Walter Kasper, *Theology of Christian Marriage* (New York: The Seabury Press, 1980), pp. 31-32.
7. Many of these qualities of human love are used by Scripture to portray profound religious truths. See *Lay-Centered Church*, pp. 83-84.
8. See Kasper, pp. 1-2.
9. See *Lay-Centered Church*, pp. 92-99.
10. See CT 48-49; Charles A. Gallagher, "Matrimonial Spirituality: A Prophetic Voice In the Church," *Studies in Formative Spirituality* 6 (1985): 201-214.
11. For additional reading see: John Paul II, "Exhortation on the Family," *Origins* 11 (1981): 437-468; for the documents on the 1980 Synod on the Family, see the complete issue of *Catholic Mind* 79 (1981), February issue; the Catholic bishops of New Jersey, "Education in Human Sexuality," *Origins* 10 (1981): 669-672; for interventions in the Synod on the Family see *Origins* 9 (1980), numbers 17, 18, 20, 21; see also the series of articles on marriage and spiritual formation in *Studies in Formative Spirituality* 6 (1985).
12. See L 11:1; Ed 3:2; C 35:4; CT 47:1.
13. See *John Paul II and the Laity*, p. 137.
14. See Henri Nouwen, *Creative Ministry* (New York: Doubleday, 1971), pp. 1-20.
15. See C 35:4; CT 48:7-8; 52:1; L 11:2.
16. See C 35:4; CT 48; 52:1; Ed 3; Co 10:2.
17. See Eugene F. Lauer, "The Holiness of Marriage: Some New Perspectives From Recent Sacramental Theology," *Studies in Formative Spirituality* 6 (1985): 215-226. For further reading see the references given by the Finleys, pp. 139-142.
18. See *John Paul II and the Laity*, p. 141.
19. For a good list of family ministries see Bishop John McGann of Rockville Centre, New York, "Pastoral Message for the Family Year," *Origins* 9 (1980): 535-540; also James Young, "The Journey into Marriage," *Origins* 11 (1981): 405-412.
20. See *Lay-Centered Church*, pp. 73-79.
21. See Cardinal George Basil Hume, "Development of Marriage Teaching," *Origins* 10 (1980): 276: "The experience [of married couples] and this understanding [of the sacrament of marriage] constitute, I would suggest, an authentic *fons theologiae* from which we, the pastors, and indeed the whole church can draw."
22. See John Paul II, "Stand Up for Human Life," *Origins* 9 (1979): 280.
23. See *Lay-Centered Church*, pp. 62-89.

CHAPTER 5. OUTREACH IN SERVICE AND SOCIAL INVOLVEMENT

1. In May 1891, Leo XIII wrote *The Workers' Charter (Rerum Novarum)*; in May 1931, Pius XI wrote *The Social Order (Quadragesimo Anno)*; in May 1961,

John XXIII wrote *New Light on Social Problems (Mater et Magistra)*, and in April 1963, he wrote *Peace on Earth (Pacem in Terris)*; in December 1965, the Vatican Council promulgated *The Church in the Modern World (Gaudium et Spes)*; in March 1967, Paul VI wrote *The Development of Peoples (Populorum Progressio)*, and in 1981, John Paul II wrote *On Human Work (Laborem Exercens)*. For a fine synthesis see David Hollenbach, "Modern Catholic Teachings Concerning Justice," *The Faith That Does Justice* (New York: Paulist Press, 1977), pp. 207-231.

2. For a detailed analysis of the Church's social teaching since Leo XIII, see Joseph Gremillion, *The Gospel of Peace and Justice* (New York: Orbis Books, 1976), pp. 3-138; see also John Coleman, "Development of Church Social Teaching," *Origins* 11 (1981): 33-41.
3. Yves Congar, *Lay People in the Church* (Westminster, Maryland: Newman Press, 1957), pp. 414-415.
4. See Leonard Doohan, *Luke: The Perennial Spirituality* (Santa Fe: Bear and Co., 1982), p. 197; Jacques Dupont, "Community of Goods in the Early Church," *The Salvation of the Gentiles* (New York: Paulist Press, 1979), pp. 85-102.
5. See *Luke: The Perennial Spirituality*, ch. 7: "Universal Concerns."
6. See U.S. Bishops' National Advisory Council, "The Thrust of Lay Ministry," *Origins* 9 (1980): 623; also O'Meara, *Theology of Ministry*, p. 20.
7. See Doohan, *The Lay-Centered Church*, pp. 4-23.
8. See *John Paul II and the Laity*, p. 8.
9. See *John Paul II and the Laity*, pp. 8-14; Synod of Bishops, *Vocation and Mission*, Nos. 22-24.
10. For the relationship between the laity's commitment to the world and their spiritual growth, see *Vocation and Mission*, Nos. 39-45; CT 4:2; 25:3; 37:5; 53:1; L 7:4; C 35:4.
11. See M 36:2; CT 43:4; 75:7.
12. *John Paul II and the Laity*, p. 11.
13. See CT 53-61.
14. See U.S. Bishops' Committee on the Parish, "The Parish: A People, a Mission, a Structure," *Origins* 10 (1981): 645.
15. See John Paul II, *Rich in Mercy (Dives in Misericordia)*, *Origins* 10 (1980): 403, 412-415.
16. Synod of Bishops, *Justice in the World* (Washington, D.C.: USCC Publications Office, 1972), p. 34.
17. See CT 40-44, 86.
18. See *John Paul II and the Laity*, pp. 48-51.
19. See CT ch. 5; *John Paul II and the Laity*, ch. 2; pp. 25-53; bishops' letter: *The Challenge of Peace*.
20. Katherine Marie Dyckman and L. Patrick Carroll, *Inviting the Mystic, Supporting the Prophet* (New York: Paulist Press, 1981), p. 83; see also Kinast, *Caring for Society*, pp. 99-115.
21. See Matthew Fox, *A Spirituality Named Compassion*, p. 8.
22. See Richard J. Mouw, "The Corporate Calling of the Laity," *The New Laity*, Ralph D. Bucy, ed. (Waco, Texas: Word Books, 1978), pp. 103-119.
23. See *Lay-Centered Church*, pp. 26-38.

CHAPTER 6. CELEBRATIONS AND LITURGICAL LIFE

1. See Doohan, "A Joyful Church," *Luke: The Perennial Spirituality*, pp. 199–201.
2. The word *liturgy* comes from the Greek words *laos ergon* meaning "the work of the people."
3. See James Dallen, *Gathering for Eucharist* (Nashville: Pastoral Arts Associates of North America, 1982), pp. 29–35.
4. For other aspects of daily life that are excellent preparations for prayer, see Leonard Doohan, "Contemplation, Authority and Obedience," *Review for Religious* 36 (1977): 572–573.
5. Hans urs von Balthasar, *Prayer*, (London: Geoffrey Chapman, 1963), p. 82; see also *John Paul II and the Laity*, pp. 85–87.
6. For definitions and explanations of the stages and types of prayer, see Agnes Cunningham, "Forms of Prayer in Christian Spirituality," *Chicago Studies* 15 (1976): 89–104; Josef Sudbrack, "Prayer," *Sacramentum Mundi*, vol. 5, Karl Rahner, ed. (New York: Herder and Herder, 1972), pp. 74–81.
7 This close connection between prayer and self-realization is true even in the later stages of prayer. See Leonard Doohan, "Personal Fulfillment in the Life and Teachings of John of the Cross," to be published in 1986 in *Contemplative Review*.
8. See Jon Sobrino, "Christian Prayer and New Testament Theology: A Basis for Social Justice and Spirituality," *Western Spirituality*, Matthew Fox, ed. (Santa Fe: Bear and Co., 1981), p. 77.
9 See Doohan, *Lay-Centered Church*, pp. 105–106.
10. Note the community call of the Second Vatican Council: M 2:3; CT 24:1; 32:1; 38:2; C 9:1, 6.
11. For the basic characteristics of community, see Evelyn Eaton Whitehead and James D. Whitehead, *Community of Faith* (New York: The Seabury Press, 1982), p. 50.
12. Regarding the basic questions of group life see Whiteheads, *Community of Faith*, p. 34.
13. The request for participation in the group's life is seen in the early decades of the Church. See Heb. 10:24–25: "Let us be concerned for each other, to stir a response in love and good works. Do not stay away from the meetings of the community, as some do, but encourage each other to go; the more so as you see the Day drawing near." Also *Epistle of Barnabas*, in *Early Christian Writings* (Harmondsworth: Penguin, 1968), p. 197: "All the same, you are not to withdraw into yourselves and live in solitude, as though God had already pronounced you holy. Come and take your full share in the meetings, and in deliberating for the common good."
14. See C 13:3; CT 12:5; 24:1.

15. Fox, A *Spirituality Named Compassion*, p. 40.
16. See Whiteheads, *Community of Faith*, ch. 2: "Clarifying the Meaning of Community."
17. Murphy, "On Parish Councils and Lay Ministry," p. 651.
18. See Doohan, *Lay-Centered Church*, pp. 47–49; also James D. Whitehead and Evelyn Eaton Whitehead, *Method in Ministry: Theological Reflection and Christian Ministry* (New York: The Seabury Press, 1980); "Ministering to the Sense of the Faithful," *Community of Faith*, pp. 153–170.
19. See "Lay Groups as Organic Communities to Better Serve the Church," *John Paul II and the Laity*, pp. 62–68.
20. Avery Dulles, *A Church to Believe In*, p. 75.
21. See Doohan, *Lay-Centered Church*, pp. 101–102.
22. See *John Paul II and the Laity*, pp. 82–87.
23. See Exodus 19:4–7; 1 Pet. 2:4–10; and Thomas W. Gillespie, "The Laity in Biblical Perspective," *Theology Today* 36 (1979–80): 315–327.
24. See Dallen, "The Assembly as Celebrant," *Gathering for Eucharist* pp. 29–35; also Bishop James Hickey, "The Sunday Liturgy in the Parish," *Origins* 9 (1980): 591. Regarding some of the Vatican Council's comments on active participation, see Lit 10; 48; C 10:2; P 6:8; M 15:2; 19:2; L 3:1.
25. James Dallen, "Spirituality of Eucharistic Prayer," *Worship* 58 (1984): 371.
26. Eugene A. Walsh, *The Ministry of the Celebrating Community* (Glendale, Arizona: Pastoral Arts Associates of North America, 1977).
27. Dallen, "Eucharistic Prayer," pp. 367–370.
28. See John Grabner, "Ordained and Lay: Them-Us or We?" *Worship* 54 (1980): 325–331.
29. See Hickey, "Sunday Liturgy," p. 593.
30. See U.S. Bishops' Ad Hoc Committee on the Parish, "Dimensions of Parish Renewal," *Origins* 9 (1980): 568.
31. See Camille D'Arienzo, "Preaching: A Ministry in Distress," *America* 143 (1980): 387–389.
32. Regarding practices in the early Church and the early development of official ministries, see Schillebeeckx, "The Christian Community and Its Office Bearers," pp. 95–133; O'Meara, *Theology of Ministry*, pp. 95–128; Bausch, *Traditions, Tensions, Transitions in Ministry*, pp. 27–61.
33. See Philip M. King, "Learning from the Laity." *Theology Today* 36 (1979–80): 368–374.

BIBLIOGRAPHY

Auer, Alfons. *Open to the World*. Dublin: Gill and Son, 1966.
Ballinger, Philip A. *The Ecclesiological Reality of "Reception."* Katholieke Universiteit Leuven, 1984.
Balthasar, Hans urs von. *Prayer*. London: Geoffrey Chapman, 1963.
Barreiro, Alvaro. *Basic Ecclesial Communities: The Evangalization of the Poor*. New York: Orbis Books, 1982.
Barta, Russell, ed. *Challenge to the Laity*. Huntington, Indiana: Our Sunday Visitor, 1980.
Bausch, William J. *Traditions, Tensions, Transitions in Ministry*. Mystic, Connecticut: Twenty-Third Publications, 1982.
Besret, Bernard. *Tomorrow a New Church*. New York: Paulist Press, 1973.
Blake, Howard C. "Styles in Christian Mission." *The New Laity*. Ralph D. Bucy, ed. Waco, Texas: Word Books, 1978, pp. 177–191.
Bleisten, Roman. "Leisure." *Sacramentum Mundi*. Vol. III, Karl Rahner and others, eds. New York: Herder and Herder, 1968, pp. 299–304.
Brown, Raymond E. *New Testament Essays*. New York: Image Books, 1968.
Bucy, Ralph D. ed. *The New Laity*. Waco, Texas: Word Books, 1978.
Catholic bishops of New Jersey. "Education in Human Sexuality." *Origins* 10 (1981): 669–672.
Chenu, M. D. *The Theology of Work*. Dublin: Gill and Son, 1963.
Church, Labor Management Dialogue in Charlotte, N.C. "The Workbench of Life." *Origins* 13 (1984): 593–602.
Code of Canon Law (Latin-English Edition). Washington, D.C.: Canon Law Society of America, 1983.
Coleman, John A. "Toward a Church with a Worldly Vocation." *Challenge to the Laity*, Russell Barta, ed. Huntington, Indiana: Our Sunday Visitor, 1980, pp. 75–105.
——— "Development of Church Social Teachings." *Origins* 11 (1981): 33–41.
Congar, Yves. *Lay People in the Church*. Westminster, Maryland: Newman Press, 1957.
Coriden, James A. "Options for the Organization of Ministry." *Jurist* 41 (1981): 480–501.
——— "The Contours of Ministry in the Eighties." *Social Thought*. Fall (1980): 3–9.
Cox, Harvey. *The Feast of Fools*. New York: Harper and Row, 1970.

Cunningham, Agnes. "Forms of Prayer in Christian Spirituality." *Chicago Studies* 15 (1976): 89–104.
Dallen, James. *Gathering for Eucharist*. Nashville: Pastoral Arts Associates of North America, 1982.
——— "Spirituality of Eucharistic Prayer." *Worship* 58 (1984): 359–372.
D'Arienzo, Camille. "Preaching: A Ministry in Distress." *America* 143 (1980): 387–389.
Dixon, Robert C., and Dean R. Hoge. "Models and Priorities of the Catholic Church as Held by Suburban Laity." *Review of Religious Research* 20 (1979): 150–167.
Doohan, Helen. *Paul and Leadership*. Wilmington, Delaware: Michael Glazier, Inc., 1984.
Doohan, Leonard. "Contemplation, Authority and Obedience." *Review for Religious* 36 (1977). 565–575.
——— "The Spiritual Value of Leisure." *Spirituality Today* 31 (1979): 157–167.
——— *Luke: The Perennial Spirituality*. Santa Fe, New Mexico: Bear and Co., 1982.
——— *The Lay-Centered Church*. Minneapolis: Winston Press, 1984.
——— *John Paul II and the Laity*. (New York: Le Jacq Publishing, Inc., 1984.
——— "Personal Fulfillment in the Life and Teachings of St. John of the Cross." *Contemplative Review* (1986).
Dosh, Terrence. "Clericalism." *Ministries* 2 (Oct. 1981): 20–23.
Dulles, Avery. *Models of the Church*. New York: Doubleday and Co., Inc., 1974.
——— *The Resilient Church*. New York: Doubleday and Co., Inc., 1977.
——— "Imaging the Church for the 1980s." *Thought* 56 (1981): 121–138.
——— *A Church to Believe In*. New York: Crossroad, 1982.
Dyckman, Katherine Marie and L. Patrick Carroll. *Inviting the Mystic, Supporting the Prophet*. New York: Paulist Press, 1981.
Finley, Mitch and Kathy. *Christian Families in the Real World*. Chicago: The Thomas More Press, 1984.
Fitzgerald, Edward. "A Time for Play?" *Clergy Review* 59 (1974): 283–292, 333–339, 400–409, 490–498, 599–565.
Fox, Matthew. "Teaching the Spirituality of Jesus: A Vision and a Blueprint." National Conference of Diocesan Directors of Religious Education, 1975, duplicated notes.
——— *Whee! We, Wee, All the Way Home: A Guide to the New Sensual Spirituality*. Santa Fe: Bear and Co., 1976.
——— *A Spirituality Named Compassion*. Minneapolis: Winston Press, 1979.

Gallagher, Charles A. "Matrimonial Spirituality: A Prophetic Voice in the Church." *Studies in Formative Spirituality* 6 (1985): 201–214.
Geaney, Dennis, "Layman Directs College's Pastoral Ministry." *National Catholic Reporter*, 19 January 1979, p. 7.
────── *Full Church, Empty Rectory.* Notre Dame, Indiana: Fides/Claretian, 1980.
Grabner, John. "Ordained and Lay: Them-Us or We?" *Worship* 54 (1980): 325–331.
Granfield, Patrick. "The Local Church as a Center of Communication and Control." *Catholic Theological Society of American Proceedings* 35 (1980): 256–263.
Greeley, Andrew, Mary Durkin, and others. *Parish, Priest and People.* Chicago: The Thomas More Press, 1981.
Gremillion, Joseph. *The Gospel of Peace and Justice.* New York: Orbis Books, 1976.
Guitton, Jean. *The Church and the Laity.* New York: Alba House, 1965.
Haight, Roger D. "Mission: The Symbol for Understanding the Church Today." *Theological Studies* 37 (1976): 620–649.
Hickey, Bishop James. "The Sunday Liturgy in The Parish." *Origins* 9 (1980): 589–604.
Hollenbach, David. "Modern Catholic Teachings Concerning Justice." *The Faith That Does Justice.* New York: Paulist Press, 1977.
Hume, George Basil, Cardinal. "Development of Marriage Teaching." *Origins* 10 (1980): 275–276.
John Paul II, Pope. "Redeemer of Man." *Origins* 8 (1979): 625–644.
────── "Work and Prayer: A Necessary Alliance in the Soul." *Origins* 9 (1979): 71–72.
────── "Stand Up for Human Life." *Origins* 9 (1979): 277–284.
────── "Apostolic Exhortation on the Family." *Origins* 11 (1981): 437–468.
────── "Synod on the Family Begins." *Origins* 10 (1980): 257–260.
────── "Rich in Mercy." *Origins* 10 (1980): 401–416.
────── "The Vatican and Its Employees." *Origins* 12 (1982): 418–421.
────── "On Human Work." *Origins* 11 (1981): 225–244.
Jones, Arthur. "Bishops: Laity Invisible to the World." *National Catholic Reporter*, 30 March 1979, pp. 12, 16.
Kasper, Walter. *Theology of Marriage.* New York: The Seabury Press, 1980.
Kilian, Sabbas J. "The Meaning and Nature of Local Church." *Catholic Theological Society of America Proceedings* 35 (1980): 244–255.
Kilmartin, Edward John. "Episcopal Election: The Right of the Laity." *Concilium* 137 (1980): 39–43.

——— "Lay Participation in the Apostolate of the Hierarchy." *Jurist* 41 (1981): 343–370.
Kinast, Robert L. *Caring for Society: A Theological Interpretation of Lay Ministry.* Chicago: The Thomas More Press, 1985.
King, Philip M. "Learning from the Laity." *Theology Today* 36 (1979–80): 368–374.
Komonchak, Joseph. "Clergy, Laity, and the Church's Mission in the World." *Jurist* 41 (1981): 422–447.
Küng, Hans. "Participation of the Laity in Church Leadership and in Church Elections." *Journal of Ecumenical Studies* 6 (1969): 511–533.
Larkin, Ernest, ed. *Spiritual Renewal of American Priesthood.* Washington, D.C.: USCC, 1973.
Lasch, Kenneth E. "Personnel Issues." *Code, Community, Ministry.* James H. Provost, ed. Washington, D.C.: Canon Law Society of America, 1983, pp. 69–74.
Lauer, Eugene F. "The Holiness of Marriage: Some New Perspectives From Recent Sacramental Theology." *Studies in Formative Spirituality* 6 (1985): 215–226.
Leckey, Dolores. "What the Laity Need." *Origins* 12 (1982): 9–15.
Lobo, George, V. *Guide to Christian Living: A New Compendium of Moral Theology.* Westminster, Maryland: Christian Classics, 1984.
Marciniak, Ed. "On the Condition of the Laity." *Challenge to the Laity.* Russell Barta, ed. Huntington, Indiana: Our Sunday Visitor, 1980, pp. 29–42.
McBrien, Richard P. *Church: The Continuing Quest.* New York: Newman Press, 1970.
——— "The Nature and Use of Power in the Church." *Catholic Theological Society of America Proceedings* 37 (1982): 38–49.
McClory, Robert. "Chicago Laity Meet; Results Mixed." *National Catholic Reporter* 3 July 1981, p. 2.
McGann, John, Bishop. "Pastoral Message for the Family Year." *Origins* 9 (1980): 535–540.
Metz, Johann Baptist. *The Emergent Church.* New York: Crossroad, 1981.
——— "Base-Church and Bourgeois Religion." *Theology Digest* 29 (1981): 203–206.
Moberg, David O. "What the Graying of America Means to the Local Church." *Christianity Today* 25 (1981): 1579–1582.
Moltmann, Jürgen. "The Diaconal Church in the Context of the Kingdom of God." *Hope for the Church.* Nashville: Abingdon Press, 1979.

Mouw, Richard J. "The Corporate Calling of the Laity." *The New Laity*. Ralph D. Bucy, ed. Waco, Texas: Word Books, 1978, pp. 103–119.

Mulders, Jacques. "After the Dutch Synod." *The Month* 13 (1980): 189–194.

Murnion, Philip J. "The Parish Community: Theological Questions Arising from Attempts to Implement Vatican II." *Catholic Theological Society of America Proceedings* 36 (1981): 39–55.

Murphy, Thomas, Bishop of Great Falls–Billings. "On Parish Councils and Lay Ministry." *Origins* 11 (1982): 650–651.

Naisbitt, John. *Megatrends*. New York: Warner Books, Inc., 1982.

Nicodemus, Donald. *The Democratic Church*. Milwaukee: The Bruce Publishing Co., 1968.

Nouwen, Henri J. M. *Creative Ministry*. New York: Doubleday, 1971.

O'Connell, Laurence J. "God's Call to Humankind: Towards a Theology of Vocation." *Chicago Studies* 18 (1979): 147–159.

O'Meara, Thomas Franklin. *Theology of Ministry*. New York: Paulist Press, 1983.

Paul VI, Pope. "Address to FAO." *L'Osservatore Romano* (English Edition), 26 November 1970, pp. 6–8.

Pottmeyer, H. J. "Pastoral Service: Laity and Priest." *Theology Digest* 27 (1979): 53–59.

Power, David Noel. "The Basis for Official Ministry in the Church," *Jurist* 41 (1981): 314–342.

Provost, James H., ed. *Code, Community, Ministry*. Washington, D.C.: Canon Law Society of America, 1983.

Rademacher, William J. *Answers for Parish Councillors*. Mystic, Connecticut: Twenty-Third Publications, 1981.

Rahner, Hugo. *Man at Play*. New York: Herder and Herder, 1967.

Rahner, Karl. "The Order of Redemption Within the Order of Creation." *Mission and Grace*, vol. 1. New York: Sheed and Ward, 1963, pp. 59–113.

——— *The Shape of the Church to Come*. New York: The Seabury Press, 1974.

Reegan, Otto Ter. "The Rights of the Laity." *Concilium* 38 (1968): 17–30.

Ruether, Rosemary. *The Church Against Itself*. New York: Herder and Herder, 1967.

——— "Matters Left Unsaid." *Commonweal* 105 (1978): 112–113.

Schillebeeckx, Edward. *God the Future of Man*. New York: Sheed and Ward, 1969.

——— "The Christian Community and Its Office-Bearers." *Concilium* 133 (1980): 95–133.

―――― *Ministry.* New York: Crossroad, 1981.
Schmude, Karl G. "Towards a Lay Spirituality." *Communio* 6 (1979): 365–377.
Schreiter, Robert. "Local Theologies in the Local Church: Issues and Methods." *Catholic Theological Society of America Proceedings* 36 (1981): 96–112.
Segundo, Juan Luis. *The Community Called Church.* New York: Orbis Books, 1973.
Sobrino, Jon. "Christian Prayer and New Testament Theology: A Basis for Social Justice and Spirituality." *Western Spirituality.* Matthew Fox, ed. Santa Fe: Bear and Co., 1981, pp. 76–114.
Spong, John Shelby. "The Emerging Church: A New Form for a New Era." *Christian Century* 96 (1979): 10–16.
Sudbrack, Josef. "Prayer." *Sacramentum Mundi,* vol. 5. Karl Rahner, ed. New York: Herder and Herder, 1970, pp. 74–81.
Synod of Bishops. *Vocation and Mission of Laity in the Church and in the World Twenty Years after the Second Vatican Council.* Vatican City, 1985.
Synod on the Family. Documents of the Synod. *Catholic Mind* 79 (Feb. 1981).
―――― "Interventions in the Synod." *Origins* 9 (1980), numbers 17, 18, 20, 21.
Thomas, David. *The Prophetic Role of the Christian Family: A Proposal for the Foundational Church.* University of Notre Dame, Pre-Synod Consultation, 15–18 June 1980.
U.S. Bishops. "Called and Gifted: Catholic Laity 1980." *Origins* 10 (1980): 369–373.
―――― "The Challenge of Peace: God's Promise and Our Response." *Origins* 13 (1983): 1–32.
―――― "Catholic Social Teaching and the U.S. Economy" (First Draft). *Origins* 14 (1984): 337–383.
U.S. Bishops' Committee on the Parish. "Dimensions of Parish Renewal." *Origins* 9 (1980): 566–569.
―――― "The Parish: A People, a Mission, a Structure." *Origins* 10 (1981): 641–646.
U.S. Bishops' National Advisory Council. "The Thrust of Lay Ministry." *Origins* 9 (1980): 621–626.
Uylenbroeck, Marcel. "Lay Associations in the Church." *L'Osservatore Romano* (English edition), 18 August 1977, p. 8.
Wallace, Annetta T. "Ongoing Marriage: Maintaining the Awe." *Studies in Formative Spirituality* 6 (1985): 271–282.
Walsh, Eugene A. *The Ministry of the Celebrating Community.* Glendale,

Arizona: Pastoral Arts Associates of North America, 1977.
Whitehead, Evelyn Eaton and James D. "Sexuality and Intimacy in Marriage." *Chicago Studies* 18 (1979): 251–261.
——— *Method in Ministry: Theological Reflection and Christian Ministry.* New York: The Seabury Press, 1980.
——— *Community of Faith.* New York: The Seabury Press, 1982.
Young, James. "The Journey into Marriage." *Origins* 11 (1981): 405–412.
Zikmund, Barbara Brown. "Christian Vocation—in Context." *Theology Today* 36 (1979–80): 328–337.

INDEX

Authority, 3, 9, 15, 16, 18, 19, 21, 33, 41, 44, 46, 65, 78, 79

Baptism, 6, 20, 94, 96, 97, 98; baptismal responsibilities, 41, 45, 66, 71, 78, 81, 85, 100, 101, 103, 122, 124; baptismal rights, 11; baptismal vocation, 11, 12, 23, 56, 94, 95, 101; dignity of, 40
Basic ecclesial communities, 5, 21, 27, 38, 39, 41, 43, 103, 121, 127
Bishops, 17, 20, 26, 31, 32, 36, 69, 91; U.S. bishops, 10, 35, 91, 125

Charisms, 29, 44, 45, 46, 98
Chenu, Marie-Dominique, 48
Chicago Declaration of Christian Concern, 7, 8
Church, domestic, 27, 30, 37, 38, 72, 73, 81, 86, 87; foundational, 27, 28, 38, 40, 41, 43, 44, 45, 72, 85, 87; lay-centered, 2, 4, 5, 12, 13, 19, 21, 38, 64, 67, 69, 92, 99, 103, 108, 109, 127; local, 2, 21, 22, 25, 26, 27, 34, 37, 72, 99; structures of, 14, 17, 18, 23; understandings of, 4, 12; universal, 26, 28, 29, 37, 40, 41, 72, 89. *See also* Models of church
Code of Canon Law, 10, 11
Collaboration, 20, 23, 30, 33, 35, 36, 67, 96, 100
Collegiality, 29, 30, 35, 43, 44, 65
Compassion, 67, 95, 96
Congar, Yves, 48
Conscience, 42, 63, 66, 69, 81, 82, 93
Consensus of the faithful, 18, 84
Constantine, 31
Consultation, 19
Conversion, 24, 25, 91, 93, 95, 110, 119, 120
Coresponsibility, 20, 21, 33, 36, 38, 44, 45, 46, 88, 89

Decision making, 9, 63, 71, 84, 85, 87

Diocese, 27, 31, 32, 38, 42
Discipleship, 11, 21
Domestic church. *See* Church
Drinan, Robert, 17
Dulles, Avery, 18, 19

Ecumenical, 43, 44, 91
Education, 6, 81, 83, 88, 89, 93, 99, 106; religious, 19, 21, 80, 125
Eschatology, 49
Evangelical counsels, 6, 96
Evangelization, 46, 64, 72, 78, 100, 104, 105

Faith, 12, 19, 33, 37, 39, 48, 50, 52, 61, 62, 78, 79, 86, 91, 96, 101, 102, 106, 107, 109, 120; faith sharing, 14, 21, 30, 39, 40, 120
Family, 6, 11, 37, 39; family life, 33, 70, 105, 116, 119
Feminism, 3, 102
Francis of Assisi, 110
Francis of Sales, 110

Hierarchy, 13, 28
Hope, 15, 21, 22, 23, 55, 104, 106, 109

John XXIII, Pope, 24, 92, 93
John Paul II, Pope, 10, 24, 27, 28, 29, 39, 55, 56, 65, 90, 92, 100

Küng, Hans, 17

Laity, relationship to hierarchy, 3, 16; rights, 11; role of, 3, 4, 7, 48, 99; theologies of, 5; unique contribution of, 25, 99, 101
Layolate. *See also* Ministry; lay
Lay Ministries. *See* Ministry of laity
Leadership, 29, 30, 31, 38, 43, 99, 108, 122, 125, 126; charismatic, 29, 30; lay, 7, 9, 18, 44, 101; pastoral, 34, 91, 125; religious, 15, 41, 85
Leckey, Dolores, 20

Leisure, 55, 58, 59, 60, 61, 62, 63, 66
Leo I, Pope, 31
Leo XIII, Pope, 55, 90, 92
Liturgy, 33, 35, 45, 64, 81, 111, 112, 113, 117, 120, 122, 123, 124, 126

Magisterium of the church, 17
Mansour, Agnes Mary, 17
Marciniak, Ed., 50
Materialism, 50
Ministry, 13, 19, 25, 29, 41, 98, 99; control of, 9, 14; family, 11, 14, 79, 86, 87; full-time, 5, 14, 79, 98; inter-vocational, 5, 21; part-time, 5, 14; prophetical, 123; social, 79, 99, 102, 103; team, 34, 45
Ministry of laity, 3, 7, 8, 9, 53, 97, 102
Mission, of Church, 2, 64, 76, 100, 111; of Christ, 101, 123; of laity, 4, 42, 54, 67
Models of church, 4, 6, 24, 25, 88; as family, 6, 37, 88; as institution, 23, 24
Moltmann, Jürgen, 36

Naisbitt, John, 10, 28
National Center for Laity, 8

Organization of Laity, 3, 7; ecclesiastical, 102; international, 3; national, 3, 8

Parish, 10, 27, 35, 37, 38, 42, 45, 112, 127
Pastoral associates, 3, 35
Pastoral leaders, 91, 113, 125
Pastoral practice, 84
Paul VI, Pope, 24, 92
Peace, 1, 13
Pius XI, Pope, 48, 92
Pluralism, 1, 5, 29, 40, 46
Politics, 99, 106, 107
Political action, 91, 97
Political involvement, 6, 65, 92, 101, 103
Polarization, 16, 18, 79
Prayer, 38, 78, 81, 84, 88, 111, 113, 115, 116, 117, 118, 120, 121, 122, 124, 126
Priests, 11, 12, 19, 20, 22, 26, 30, 31, 32, 33, 34, 38, 39, 40, 44, 58, 68, 69, 72, 79, 85, 88, 108, 109, 116, 126; shortage of, 3, 4, 13, 35, 39, 41, 46, 99, 101, 108
Priesthood of all the baptized, 115

Rahner, Karl, 48
Religious, 11, 12, 20, 22, 30, 31, 34, 38, 40, 58, 68, 69, 72, 79, 85, 88, 102, 116

Sacramental life, 14, 72, 73, 74, 110, 123
Schillebeeckx, Edward, 17, 18, 30, 48
Sin, 50, 51, 66, 76, 77, 94, 95, 96, 104, 106, 118
Social justice, 88, 90, 91, 93, 96, 99, 100, 107, 108, 109; involvement, 98, 99, 101; removal of injustice, 93, 122; responsibility for, 94, 95, 96
Spiritual movements, 3, 11, 13, 14, 24, 30, 48, 71, 90, 111, 119
Spirituality, 6, 11, 19, 24, 46, 66, 72, 73, 75, 104, 112, 115, 123, 124, 126; family, 69, 77, 86; lay, 23, 49; of marriage, 46, 86; of work, 49
Structures of the church, 14, 17, 18, 23
Subsidiarity, 44
Synod on the family, 69

Thils, Gustave, 48

Vatican Council II, 2, 11, 15, 20, 23, 24, 25, 32, 33, 34, 43, 48, 50, 76, 83, 100, 111, 114, 123; developments since, 7, 13, 16, 69, 125; reactions since, 1, 2, 22
Vocation, 51, 53, 54, 86

Women, 16, 17, 19, 41, 66, 70, 71, 77, 88, 90, 101, 102, 108, 110
World, autonomy of, 48, 51, 104; consecration of, 51, 67; development of, 51

www.ingramcontent.com/pod-product-compliance
Lightning Source LLC
Chambersburg PA
CBHW072142160426
43197CB00012B/2215